Table of Contents

1 Chapter 1: Event Formation

The foundation of any successful interstellar sporting event lies in the meticulous planning and execution of the initial formation stages. This involves establishing the Galactic Games Committee (GGC), a governing body responsible for overseeing all aspects of the event. The GGC should be composed of representatives from various member planets, each possessing expertise in different areas like logistics, finance, regulations, and public relations. A clear hierarchical structure within the committee is essential, defining roles and responsibilities to ensure smooth operation. Consider establishing sub-committees dedicated to specific tasks, such as venue selection, participant management, and security. This compartmentalization allows for focused attention on each critical area, promoting efficiency and accountability. Regular communication and reporting mechanisms within the GGC are crucial for maintaining transparency and coordinating efforts effectively.

Choosing individuals to fill these roles requires careful consideration of their experience and qualifications. Seek out individuals with proven track records in event management, preferably on a large scale, though interstellar experience is naturally scarce. Look for diplomatic skills and the ability to navigate intercultural sensitivities, vital in a galaxy of diverse species and customs. Technical expertise is also a valuable asset, especially in areas like interstellar communication and advanced logistics. Thorough background checks and vetting procedures are recommended to ensure the integrity and competence of committee members. Once selected, provide comprehensive training on the specific regulations and protocols relevant to the Galactic Games. This will empower them to make informed decisions and uphold the highest standards of fairness and ethical conduct.

A realistic budget is the backbone of any successful event. Begin by conducting a comprehensive needs assessment, identifying all potential expenses. This encompasses everything from venue rental and construction to security personnel and broadcasting equipment. Factor in the unique challenges of interstellar events, such as specialized transportation and accommodation for diverse species. Once you've established a comprehensive list of expenses, explore various funding sources. Secure sponsorship deals with interstellar corporations, negotiate subsidies from participating planetary governments, and explore options for merchandise and broadcasting rights sales. Develop a detailed budget plan that outlines projected income and expenses, allowing for contingency funds to address unforeseen circumstances. Regular budget reviews throughout the planning process are essential to ensure fiscal responsibility and adapt to evolving needs.

Budget planning for a galactic-scale event requires foresight and meticulous attention to detail. Consider the fluctuating exchange rates of various interstellar currencies and establish a standardized currency for all transactions to simplify financial management. Implement transparent accounting practices and establish a system for tracking all expenditures. Explore the use of blockchain technology to ensure secure and transparent financial record-keeping. Engage independent auditors to verify financial reports, enhancing credibility and accountability. Transparency in financial matters fosters trust among stakeholders, including sponsors, participants, and the galactic community at large. This meticulous approach to financial management is crucial for the long-term sustainability of the Galactic Games.

Establishing a robust communication framework is paramount. Create a dedicated communication channel for the GGC, allowing for real-time updates and information sharing. This could involve secure interstellar communication networks or dedicated holographic meeting platforms. Regular meetings should be scheduled to discuss progress, address challenges, and make collective decisions. Clear communication protocols should be established to ensure efficient dissemination of information to all relevant parties. This includes participants, sponsors, media outlets, and the general public. Consider establishing a dedicated website or online portal to serve as a central hub for information related to the Games. This will provide easy access to schedules, rules, and updates, fostering transparency and engagement with the galactic community.

Finally, anticipate potential challenges and develop contingency plans to address them. Interstellar events are inherently complex, involving numerous variables that can impact the smooth execution of the Games. Develop protocols for dealing with unforeseen circumstances, such as planetary emergencies, political instability, or unexpected participant withdrawals. Establish a crisis management team equipped to handle any situation that may arise, ensuring the safety and well-being of all involved. By proactively addressing potential challenges, you can minimize disruptions and maintain the integrity of the Galactic Games. This careful planning will not only contribute to the success of the current event but also lay a solid foundation for future interstellar sporting spectacles.

1.1 Initial Setup

The first step in organizing any interstellar sporting event under the Galactic Games Committee (GGC) banner is establishing a robust organizational structure. This involves more than simply gathering interested individuals; it requires a methodical approach to define roles, responsibilities, and communication pathways. Begin by creating a core committee. This central body should include representatives from key areas: logistics, regulations, finance, security, and public relations. Each member should possess a demonstrable expertise in their respective field, along with a deep understanding of the unique challenges posed by interstellar events. Consider past experience organizing large-scale gatherings, ideally with multispecies participation. Diversity of thought and perspective is crucial.

Once the core committee is formed, clearly define their individual roles and responsibilities. A detailed charter should be drafted, outlining each member's authority, reporting structure, and decision-making power. This document will serve as the foundation for all future operations, mitigating potential conflicts and ensuring smooth collaboration. Include specific procedures for conflict resolution within the charter, anticipating disagreements that might arise during the planning process. These procedures should involve a tiered approach, beginning with mediation within the committee and escalating to arbitration by a neutral third party if necessary. Detailed records of all committee meetings, decisions, and communications should be meticulously maintained, forming a comprehensive archive of the event's development.

Next, establish clear communication protocols within the committee. Given the vast distances and potential for communication delays across interstellar space, a reliable and efficient system is paramount. Real-time communication platforms, utilizing advanced subspace transceivers, should be employed for immediate exchanges. These systems must be secure, encrypted, and accessible to all committee members regardless of their location within the galaxy. Backup communication channels should also be established in the event of primary system failure, perhaps through a network of secure relay stations positioned strategically across different sectors. Regularly scheduled meetings, both virtual and in-person where feasible, should be established to maintain momentum and ensure consistent progress. These meetings provide a forum for discussing updates, addressing challenges, and making collective decisions. The frequency and format of these meetings should be clearly outlined in the committee charter.

Simultaneously, the committee must develop a comprehensive timeline. This timeline will serve as a roadmap for all subsequent planning stages, dictating deadlines, milestones, and key deliverables. Break down the overall event planning process into smaller, manageable tasks, assigning specific responsibilities and due dates for each. This detailed timeline should be accessible to all committee members, facilitating transparency and accountability. Incorporate buffer time into the schedule to accommodate unforeseen delays or complications. The inherent complexities of interstellar travel, communication, and logistics necessitate a degree of flexibility.

Consider, for example, the registration process for participating teams. This process should begin well in advance of the event itself, allowing ample time for teams to assemble, submit the necessary documentation, and secure travel arrangements. The registration portal should be accessible across the galaxy, utilizing a standardized format and language protocol to accommodate diverse species. Clear guidelines regarding eligibility criteria, team composition, and required documentation should be readily available. Develop a tiered system for handling registration inquiries and issues, ensuring prompt and efficient responses to queries from prospective participants. This may involve dedicated support staff fluent in various galactic languages.

Furthermore, the initial setup phase requires a preliminary assessment of potential venues. While the detailed selection process will be addressed in a later chapter, an early evaluation of potential host planets is crucial. This initial assessment should focus on fundamental criteria such as atmospheric compatibility, gravitational stability, and available infrastructure. A preliminary list of suitable candidates should be compiled, considering factors such as accessibility, political stability, and cultural receptiveness to hosting a large-scale interstellar event. This preliminary list will serve as a starting point for the more in-depth venue selection process. Gathering data on potential locations necessitates collaboration with planetary authorities, requiring diplomatic efforts and careful consideration of interstellar protocols.

Finally, establish a preliminary budget. This initial budget should serve as a working document, subject to revision as the planning process progresses and more concrete data becomes available. It should include estimated costs for venue rental, infrastructure development, security measures, participant travel and accommodation, broadcasting rights, and marketing campaigns. Explore potential revenue streams, including sponsorship agreements, merchandise sales, and broadcasting rights licensing. Developing a realistic budget is crucial for securing the necessary financial resources and ensuring the long-term sustainability of the event. This requires careful analysis of market trends, sponsorship opportunities, and projected revenue streams. Flexibility and adaptability are essential, allowing for adjustments based on evolving circumstances and unexpected contingencies.

1.2 Committee Roles

A successful Galactic Games Committee requires a diverse and dedicated team, each member playing a crucial role in the event's smooth execution. These roles are interconnected and require constant communication and collaboration. Think of the committee as a complex starship, each individual operating a vital system to ensure a successful voyage.

The Chairperson acts as the ultimate authority, steering the committee and overseeing all aspects of the games. They are responsible for making final decisions, mediating disputes between committee members, and representing the Galactic Games to external stakeholders. This role demands exceptional leadership qualities, diplomatic skills, and an extensive understanding of interstellar sports and cultures. They are the captain of the ship, charting the course and ensuring the mission's success.

The Vice-Chairperson serves as the Chairperson's second-in-command, stepping in when the Chairperson is unavailable. They also take on specific responsibilities delegated by the Chairperson, often focusing on a particular area like logistics or participant relations. This individual must possess strong organizational and problem-solving abilities, acting as a reliable support system for the Chairperson.

The Secretary is responsible for all official communications and record-keeping. They manage correspondence, draft meeting minutes, maintain official documents, and ensure information flows smoothly within the committee and to external parties. Meticulous attention to detail and excellent organizational skills are essential for this role, as they are the keepers of the event's official history.

The Treasurer manages the financial aspects of the games, overseeing budgeting, sponsorship acquisition, and expenditure tracking. They develop and monitor the budget, secure funding from various sources, and ensure financial transparency throughout the event. Strong financial acumen, negotiation skills, and impeccable ethical standards are paramount for this position. They are the custodians of the games' financial resources, ensuring sustainability and responsible management.

The Head of Logistics orchestrates the intricate web of transportation, accommodation, and venue management. This involves coordinating interstellar travel for participants, securing suitable accommodation that caters to diverse species' needs, and managing the complex logistics of various sporting venues. Exceptional organizational skills, adaptability, and an understanding of interstellar travel protocols are crucial. They are the architects of movement, ensuring everyone and everything arrives where it needs to be, when it needs to be there.

The Head of Security is responsible for the safety and well-being of all participants and spectators. This encompasses developing and implementing comprehensive security protocols, coordinating with security forces from various planetary systems, and managing crowd control during the games. Experience in interspecies security measures, crisis management, and conflict resolution are essential for this role. They are the guardians of peace, ensuring a safe and secure environment for all involved.

The Head of Media and Communications manages the event's public image and outreach. They are responsible for media relations, interstellar broadcast negotiations, social media engagement, and developing marketing strategies to promote the games. Strong communication skills, media savvy, and an understanding of diverse cultural sensitivities are key. They are the storytellers, shaping the narrative and sharing the excitement of the Galactic Games with the universe.

The Head of Sports and Competition oversees all aspects related to the sporting events themselves. This includes selecting the games, adapting rules for interspecies competition, ensuring fair play, and managing dispute resolution processes. A deep understanding of various interstellar sports, strong analytical skills, and impartiality are vital. They are the guardians of fair play, ensuring the integrity and spirit of competition are upheld at all times.

The Head of Medical Services is responsible for providing comprehensive medical care to all participants and spectators. This includes setting up medical facilities, coordinating with medical personnel from various species, and establishing emergency protocols. Expertise in interspecies medicine, emergency response, and preventative care is crucial for this demanding role. They are the healers, ensuring the health and well-being of everyone involved.

These distinct roles, while specialized, must operate in a coordinated and collaborative manner. Effective communication, mutual respect, and a shared vision of a successful Galactic Games are essential for the committee to function effectively. Each member contributes a unique skill set, forming a powerful team capable of overcoming the immense challenges of organizing an interstellar sporting event. Their collective effort, like a well-oiled machine, will bring the grand vision of the Galactic Games to life.

1.3   Budget Planning

Effective budget planning is the bedrock of any successful interstellar sporting event. A meticulously crafted budget ensures the seamless execution of every aspect, from venue acquisition to awards ceremonies, and minimizes the risk of financial overruns. This chapter outlines a structured approach to budgeting for a galactic-scale event, providing practical guidance for the Galactic Games Committee.

Begin by meticulously itemizing all anticipated expenditures. This comprehensive list should encompass every conceivable cost, ranging from the grand scale of interstellar travel and venue construction to the minutiae of catering and medical supplies. Consider the unique needs of diverse galactic species – dietary restrictions, atmospheric requirements, and potential translation services. Factor in contingency funds for unforeseen circumstances like unexpected planetary weather patterns or emergency repairs to interstellar transport vessels. Overestimate rather than underestimate to provide a financial buffer.

Once expenditures are comprehensively outlined, explore potential revenue streams. Sponsorship from galactic corporations can be a significant source of funding. Negotiate contracts with these entities, offering tiered packages with varying levels of visibility and branding opportunities. Consider offering exclusive merchandise rights, prominent signage within the venue, and integrated advertising within interstellar broadcasts. Ticket sales, while complex given the vast distances and varying currencies, represent another revenue avenue. Implement a tiered pricing system based on seat location and access to exclusive areas, catering to diverse budgets and preferences. Merchandise sales, including apparel, memorabilia, and holographic recordings of the games, can generate further income.

A crucial step is developing a realistic timeline for both income and expenses. Map out expected sponsorship payments, ticket sales projections, and merchandise revenue timelines. Align these with the projected expenditure schedule for venue bookings, equipment rentals, and participant travel arrangements. This allows for proactive management of cash flow, ensuring funds are available when needed and avoiding potential delays or disruptions.

Regular budget monitoring and revision are essential. Track actual income and expenses against the projected figures. Identify any discrepancies and analyze the reasons behind them. Are sponsorship deals underperforming? Are ticket sales lagging behind projections? Based on this analysis, adjust the budget accordingly. This dynamic approach ensures the budget remains a relevant and effective tool throughout the event planning process.

Transparency and meticulous record-keeping are paramount. Maintain detailed records of all transactions, both income and expenses. This not only aids in accurate financial reporting but also provides valuable data for future events. Analyze the effectiveness of various revenue generation strategies and identify areas for improvement. This data-driven approach will enhance the financial viability and sustainability of future Galactic Games.

Consider establishing a dedicated finance subcommittee within the Galactic Games Committee. This team, comprised of individuals with expertise in interstellar finance and accounting, will be responsible for overseeing all financial aspects of the event. They will manage the budget, track income and expenses, negotiate sponsorship deals, and prepare financial reports. This dedicated focus ensures financial stability and accountability throughout the event lifecycle.

Negotiate favorable exchange rates with galactic banks to minimize transaction costs associated with diverse interstellar currencies. Establish secure payment gateways for ticket sales and merchandise purchases, accommodating various forms of currency and ensuring seamless transactions for participants and spectators from across the galaxy. Explore partnerships with interstellar transportation companies to secure discounted rates for participant travel, reducing logistical costs and making the games more accessible to teams from distant sectors.

Investigate potential tax implications for the event, considering the varying tax laws and regulations across different galactic jurisdictions. Ensure compliance with all relevant regulations to avoid legal complications and maintain the reputation of the Galactic Games Committee. This proactive approach demonstrates financial responsibility and builds trust with participating teams and sponsors.

Contingency planning is vital in the unpredictable realm of interstellar events. Allocate a portion of the budget specifically for unforeseen circumstances. This could include unexpected travel delays due to solar flares, emergency medical evacuations, or the need to repair damaged equipment. Having a financial buffer in place allows the committee to address these challenges swiftly and effectively without jeopardizing the event's overall success.

Finally, prioritize cost-effectiveness without compromising quality. Seek out competitive pricing for venue rentals, equipment, and services. Explore opportunities for bulk purchasing and negotiate discounts with vendors. Implement sustainable practices to minimize resource consumption and reduce environmental impact, aligning the games with responsible galactic citizenship. This mindful approach ensures the event is both financially sound and ethically responsible.

2 Chapter 2: Venue Selection

Selecting a venue for interstellar sporting events is a multifaceted endeavor, demanding careful consideration of numerous factors to ensure the safety, fairness, and overall success of the games. This process goes beyond simply choosing a planet with a large stadium; it requires a comprehensive evaluation of planetary conditions, existing infrastructure, and the specific requirements of each sport being hosted. Failing to adequately address these elements can lead to disastrous consequences, ranging from unfair competitive advantages to life-threatening situations for participants and spectators alike.

Planetary criteria form the bedrock of venue selection. Atmospheric composition is paramount. Athletes from oxygen-breathing worlds will require environments with compatible air mixtures, while species adapted to nitrogen-rich or other unique atmospheres will necessitate tailored solutions, potentially including sealed arenas or localized atmospheric adjustments. Gravity is another crucial consideration. High-gravity environments could severely disadvantage species from low-gravity worlds, while the reverse could create dangerous situations for those accustomed to stronger gravitational pulls. The stability of the planet's environment also plays a vital role. Planets prone to seismic activity, extreme weather events, or unstable atmospheric conditions pose significant risks and logistical challenges. The presence of pre-existing infrastructure, such as suitable transportation networks, accommodations, and energy sources, greatly influences the feasibility and cost-effectiveness of hosting an event on a particular planet.

Once a suitable planet has been identified, the focus shifts to the specifics of the arena itself. Arena size is determined by the sport's spatial requirements, anticipated spectator numbers, and the need for ancillary facilities like training areas and medical centers. For instance, a zero-gravity racquet sport might require a vast, enclosed space, while a ground-based contact sport could utilize a more traditional stadium design. Technological capabilities of the arena are crucial. Advanced scoring systems, environmental controls, and holographic replay technology can enhance the spectator experience and ensure fair play. Safety features, such as emergency evacuation systems, protective barriers, and advanced medical bays, are non-negotiable, especially when dealing with the diverse physiological needs of interstellar athletes. Spectator capacity must be carefully calculated based on projected attendance, incorporating factors like species-specific comfort requirements, accessibility for various body types and mobility needs, and the potential impact of large crowds on the local environment and infrastructure.

Beyond the immediate requirements of the sport and spectators, long-term sustainability and ethical considerations must be incorporated into venue selection. The environmental impact of hosting the games should be minimized by choosing locations with robust ecosystems and employing eco-friendly technologies. Respect for local cultures and traditions is paramount. The venue selection process should involve consultation with indigenous populations to ensure that the event does not disrupt existing societal structures or infringe upon cultural sensitivities. Accessibility for diverse species, both participants and spectators, is crucial. Venues should be designed to accommodate a wide range of physiological needs, including variations in size, mobility, sensory perception, and environmental tolerance. This might involve creating specialized seating areas, providing translation services, or adapting existing infrastructure to accommodate unique requirements.

Furthermore, the political stability of the host planet and its surrounding region is a key factor to consider. Hosting the games in a politically volatile area could jeopardize the safety and security of everyone involved. A thorough risk assessment should be conducted to evaluate the potential for political unrest, terrorism, or other security threats. This assessment should inform the development of comprehensive security plans and contingency measures to mitigate these risks. The availability of local security forces and their capacity to collaborate with interstellar security teams is also a vital consideration. The legal framework of the host planet should be carefully examined. Clear agreements regarding jurisdiction, liability, and intellectual property rights are necessary to avoid legal disputes and ensure a smooth operation of the games. These agreements should be negotiated with the host planet's governing body and adhere to galactic legal standards. A clear process for dispute resolution should be established, incorporating representatives from both the Galactic Games Committee and the host planet.

Finally, the financial implications of venue selection are substantial. The cost of building or modifying an arena, accommodating participants and spectators, and implementing necessary security measures can vary significantly between planets. A detailed cost-benefit analysis should be conducted to evaluate the financial viability of different venue options. Securing sponsorships and partnerships can help offset the costs, but it's essential to ensure that these agreements align with the values of the Galactic Games Committee and do not compromise the integrity of the event. The long-term economic impact on the host planet should also be considered. The games can provide a significant boost to the local economy, but it's crucial to ensure that this growth is sustainable and benefits the local population in the long run.

In conclusion, selecting a suitable venue for interstellar sporting events is a complex undertaking that requires a holistic approach. From planetary conditions to arena specifics, and from ethical considerations to financial implications, every aspect must be meticulously evaluated to ensure a successful and memorable event. By adhering to these guidelines, the Galactic Games Committee can guarantee the safety and enjoyment of participants and spectators alike, while upholding the principles of fair play and promoting intercultural understanding across the galaxy.

2.1 Planetary Criteria

Selecting a planet to host the Galactic Games is a complex undertaking. It's not simply a matter of finding a pleasant climate and a spacious arena. We must consider the physiological needs of a diverse range of athletes, the logistical challenges of interstellar travel, and the potential impact on the host planet's environment and culture. This chapter provides a comprehensive framework for evaluating planetary suitability, ensuring the safety, fairness, and overall success of the Games.

First and foremost, atmospheric composition is critical. Oxygen-breathing species, for example, require specific oxygen levels and minimal presence of toxic gases. Similarly, species adapted to methane or nitrogen-rich atmospheres will have unique requirements. A comprehensive analysis of atmospheric pressure, temperature gradients, and potential allergens is also essential. This data will inform the selection of suitable life support systems and ensure athlete comfort and performance. Remember, even slight deviations from optimal atmospheric conditions can significantly impact athletic performance and even pose health risks.

Gravitational force is another crucial factor. Species evolved under high gravity will experience significant physiological stress in low-gravity environments, and vice versa. Bone density, muscle mass, and cardiovascular function are all affected by gravity. Therefore, we must carefully match the gravitational pull of the host planet to the physiological tolerances of the participating species. This might involve selecting planets with similar gravity to the athletes' home worlds or implementing artificial gravity systems within the arena and training facilities. The latter, though technologically feasible, presents a significant logistical and financial challenge.

Beyond atmospheric and gravitational considerations, the availability of suitable infrastructure is paramount. The host planet must possess adequate transportation networks, energy resources, and communication systems. Consider the logistics of transporting athletes, equipment, and spectators across vast interstellar distances. The planet must have the capacity to handle the influx of visitors and provide them with essential amenities. This includes accommodation, food, and medical facilities capable of catering to a diverse range of physiological needs. A thorough assessment of existing infrastructure and the potential for expansion is therefore a vital component of the selection process.

Furthermore, the potential impact of the Games on the host planet's environment must be carefully evaluated. Large-scale sporting events inevitably generate waste and consume resources. We must ensure that the host planet's ecosystem can withstand the environmental pressures of the Games. This involves analyzing the planet's carrying capacity, its waste management systems, and its vulnerability to pollution. Sustainable practices, such as utilizing renewable energy sources and minimizing waste generation, are crucial to minimizing our environmental footprint. The Games should leave a positive legacy on the host planet, not a trail of environmental degradation.

Cultural sensitivity and respect for the host planet's indigenous populations are equally important. The Games should be a celebration of intergalactic unity and cultural exchange, not a source of conflict or exploitation. We must engage with local communities, respect their customs and traditions, and ensure that the Games benefit them economically and socially. This might involve collaborating with local artisans, showcasing indigenous art and culture, and investing in community development projects. Building positive relationships with the host planet's inhabitants is essential for the long-term success and sustainability of the Games.

Finally, political stability and security considerations cannot be overlooked. The host planet must have a stable political environment and robust security measures in place to ensure the safety and well-being of all participants and spectators. This includes measures to prevent terrorism, crime, and civil unrest. A thorough risk assessment should be conducted to identify potential security threats and develop appropriate mitigation strategies. Collaboration with local law enforcement agencies and intergalactic security forces will be crucial in maintaining a safe and secure environment for the Games.

Selecting a suitable host planet for the Galactic Games is a multifaceted decision, requiring a careful balance of scientific, logistical, environmental, cultural, and security considerations. By adhering to the guidelines presented in this chapter, the Galactic Games Committee can ensure that the Games are not only a spectacular display of athletic prowess but also a testament to intergalactic cooperation, sustainability, and respect for diverse cultures. This meticulous selection process will lay the foundation for a successful and memorable event for all involved. The selection process should not be rushed; ample time must be allocated to thoroughly assess each potential host planet and make an informed decision that benefits the Games and the host planet alike. This is not simply about finding a venue; it's about fostering intergalactic harmony and promoting the spirit of sportsmanship throughout the galaxy.

2.2   Arena Requirements

The core considerations for any interstellar sporting arena revolve around adaptability and safety. These structures must cater to a potentially vast array of species with wildly differing physiological needs, while simultaneously ensuring the integrity of the competition and the well-being of all attendees. Therefore, modularity is paramount. Arena floors should be capable of rapid reconfiguration, shifting gravity, atmospheric composition, and even temperature to suit the specific requirements of each sport and the competing species. Consider, for instance, a low-gravity aerial sport played by a species that breathes methane. The arena must be capable of seamlessly transitioning from standard gravity and oxygenated air to the necessary low-gravity environment and methane-rich atmosphere. This dynamic adaptability requires advanced technological integration and robust environmental control systems.

Beyond atmospheric and gravitational considerations, arena dimensions themselves need to be adaptable. Some sports might require vast, open spaces, while others might call for more confined arenas. Imagine a sport played by colossal beings; the arena must expand to accommodate their immense size and the scope of their movements. Conversely, a sport involving intricate maneuvers and high speeds might necessitate a smaller, more contained environment. This flexibility can be achieved through movable walls, retractable seating, and even holographic boundaries that can be adjusted to define the playing field according to the specific needs of each event. These adjustments should be swift and seamless, minimizing downtime between competitions and maximizing the use of the arena. Spectator comfort and safety are also crucial factors. Seating arrangements must accommodate diverse body types, sizes, and sensory preferences. Some species might require specialized seating that caters to their unique physiology, such as anti-gravity harnesses for floating species or temperature-controlled enclosures for those sensitive to extreme temperatures. Sensory accommodations are equally important. Lighting, sound levels, and even ambient smells must be adjustable to prevent overstimulation or distress among spectators from different sensory backgrounds. Furthermore, clear lines of sight and optimal viewing angles should be ensured for all spectators, regardless of their physical location within the arena. This might involve holographic projection systems that provide personalized viewpoints or strategically placed viewing platforms that cater to different heights and perspectives.

The integration of advanced technology is essential for facilitating fair play and enhancing the spectator experience. Real-time data analysis and holographic replays can provide instant insights into game dynamics, offering spectators a deeper understanding of the competition. These systems can also assist referees in making accurate calls and ensuring the integrity of the game. Moreover, personalized data feeds can be streamed directly to spectators, allowing them to access player statistics, historical data, and even real-time physiological information about the athletes. This immersive experience deepens engagement and connects spectators to the event in unprecedented ways.

Security measures within the arena must be comprehensive and adaptable to various threats and emergencies. Consider the possibility of rogue drones, disruptive technologies, or even interspecies conflicts. The arena should be equipped with advanced security systems that can detect and neutralize these threats swiftly and effectively. This includes sophisticated scanning technology, energy shields, and even specialized security personnel trained to handle interspecies conflicts and diffuse tense situations. Moreover, the arena's design should incorporate multiple escape routes and emergency exits strategically placed throughout the venue. These exits should be clearly marked and easily accessible to all attendees, regardless of their species or physical abilities. Regular drills and simulations should be conducted to ensure that all personnel and spectators are familiar with evacuation procedures in the event of an emergency.

Environmental controls within the arena must extend beyond the playing field. Spectator areas should maintain comfortable temperatures and atmospheric conditions suitable for a diverse range of species. Dedicated areas for species with specific environmental needs, such as high-humidity zones or low-gravity chambers, should be readily available. Furthermore, waste management systems must be in place to handle the unique byproducts of different species, ensuring a clean and sanitary environment for all attendees. These systems should prioritize sustainability and minimize the environmental impact of the event.

Finally, accessibility is a critical consideration. The arena should be designed to accommodate individuals with disabilities, regardless of their species. This includes providing ramps, elevators, and other assistive technologies to ensure that all attendees can navigate the venue with ease. Sensory accommodations for individuals with sensory sensitivities should also be available, such as quiet rooms, designated areas with reduced lighting, and assistive listening devices. By prioritizing accessibility, the Galactic Games Committee demonstrates its commitment to inclusivity and ensures that all members of the galactic community can participate in and enjoy the interstellar sporting events.

3 Chapter 3: Sports & Regulations

The Galactic Games Committee faces a unique challenge: selecting sports suitable for interstellar competition. Consider the Gravitational Tilt, a sport played on platforms suspended within a controlled gravity field. Teams manipulate the field's intensity and direction to navigate a complex obstacle course. However, species accustomed to high gravity might have a significant advantage, necessitating careful balancing of the gravitational parameters. Alternatively, the Zero-G Orb Relay, played in a weightless environment, requires participants to strategically pass energized orbs through a series of designated gates. This sport levels the playing field for species with varying physical capabilities but presents challenges in standardizing orb propulsion techniques across different limb structures. Choosing appropriate sports demands careful consideration of species-specific advantages and disadvantages, with an emphasis on creating a balanced and engaging competitive environment.

Once the games are selected, adapting the rules for interspecies competition becomes paramount. Take, for example, the Sonic Skirmish, a game involving projectiles launched using sonic pulses. Species with sensitive auditory systems might be unfairly disadvantaged. Adjustments like dampening sonic frequencies or providing auditory protection could ensure equitable participation. The Crystalline Capture, a game requiring the strategic collection of energized crystals, presents another challenge. Some species might possess natural bio-electric fields that interfere with crystal energy, necessitating the development of specialized containment devices. Rule modifications must address not just physical differences, but also the unique biological and physiological attributes of competing species.

Safety protocols are critical. In the Photon Fencing competition, combatants wield beams of focused light, demanding stringent eye protection measures. Specialized visors must be designed to filter harmful radiation while allowing for clear visibility. Furthermore, the arena itself must be constructed from materials capable of containing stray photon beams, preventing accidental injuries to spectators. Similarly, in the Anti-Gravity Acrobatics competition, participants perform complex maneuvers in a zero-gravity chamber. Redundant safety nets and emergency gravity generators must be in place to mitigate the risks associated with sudden equipment malfunctions. Every chosen sport requires a bespoke safety plan.

Disputes, inevitably, will arise. The Galactic Games Committee must establish clear procedures for resolving them. Consider a scenario where a player in the Neural Net Race, a mental competition conducted within a virtual reality space, is accused of using unauthorized neural enhancements. The resolution process would require verification of the competitor's neural activity logs, potentially involving sensitive biological data. Clear protocols for data access and analysis, respecting the privacy of participants, are crucial. For physical disputes, like a contested goal in the Quantum Quidditch match, holographic replays and impartial officiating technology should be employed, providing unbiased evidence for swift and fair decision-making. Building trust in the dispute resolution process is paramount for maintaining the integrity of the games.

Doping control is a sensitive but essential aspect of interstellar competition. The use of performance-enhancing substances presents an unprecedented challenge. Imagine a species capable of naturally producing a biochemical compound that dramatically enhances speed and reflexes. Determining whether this constitutes an unfair advantage requires meticulous analysis and the establishment of clear biological baselines for each participating species. Furthermore, the detection of synthetic performance enhancers becomes exponentially more complex when dealing with the diverse biochemistries of galactic athletes. Sophisticated scanning technologies and rigorous testing protocols are essential. Implementing a comprehensive and transparent doping control program ensures fairness and preserves the integrity of the competition. This program must balance the need for rigorous enforcement with respect for the biological diversity of the galactic community. Ethical considerations must guide the development and implementation of all doping-related policies. Education on the risks of performance-enhancing substances is equally important, fostering a culture of fair play and sportsmanship throughout the galaxy.

3.1 Game Choices

The Galactic Games Committee faces a unique challenge: selecting sports that cater to a galaxy teeming with diverse species and physical capabilities. Consider the Gorthans, whose dense bone structure makes them excel at high-gravity grappling, but who struggle in low-gravity environments. Conversely, the ethereal Sylvans, masters of aerial acrobatics, find planet-bound sports challenging. Balancing these disparate needs requires a careful curation of sporting events, a delicate blend of traditional and innovative games. Zero-G Capture the Flag, for example, uses magnetized suits and a glowing orb, offering an exciting spectacle for both participants and viewers regardless of physiological differences.

This selection process begins with a comprehensive survey distributed across participating civilizations. This survey gauges interest in existing sports while also soliciting proposals for new games unique to specific species or cultures. The survey should detail necessary equipment, playing surface requirements, and any specific environmental needs. This data allows the committee to analyze the popularity and feasibility of each proposed sport, considering factors like venue adaptability and spectator appeal. This democratic approach ensures that the final selection reflects the desires of the galactic community.

Next, a rigorous evaluation process assesses the practicality of each sport. A dedicated subcommittee, comprising experts in xenobiology, sports science, and event management, scrutinizes the proposed games. They analyze the physical demands of each sport, ensuring it can be played safely by a range of species. This subcommittee also evaluates the logistical feasibility of each game, considering factors such as equipment availability, venue modifications, and potential environmental impacts. For instance, a sport involving highly volatile chemicals might be deemed too risky for a densely populated venue.

Innovation plays a crucial role in broadening the appeal of the Galactic Games. The committee actively encourages the development of new sports tailored to the unique abilities of different species. Consider the Lumina Relay, a race involving bioluminescent creatures native to a specific nebula. These creatures are passed between team members, their glowing bodies creating a mesmerizing spectacle against the backdrop of space. Such innovative games not only showcase the diversity of the galaxy but also foster interspecies understanding and collaboration.

Beyond established and novel sports, the committee explores variations of existing games adapted for interstellar competition. Gravityball, a modified version of basketball played in variable gravity environments, offers a thrilling test of adaptability and skill. Players must adjust their tactics and techniques based on the fluctuating gravitational field, adding an extra layer of complexity to the game. These adaptations not only make familiar sports more accessible to diverse species but also offer exciting new challenges for seasoned athletes.

The committee also acknowledges the importance of spectator engagement. Sports are chosen not only for their competitive value but also for their entertainment potential. Visual spectacle, strategic depth, and narrative excitement are all considered. For instance, the Cosmic Regatta, a race involving sleek, solar-powered sailboats navigating asteroid fields, offers a visually stunning spectacle for audiences across the galaxy. This emphasis on entertainment ensures that the Galactic Games become a celebrated event throughout the cosmos.

Inclusivity is paramount in the game selection process. The committee strives to include sports that can be enjoyed by participants of all skill levels and physical abilities. This includes adapted versions of popular sports with modified rules and equipment to accommodate diverse needs. For instance, a low-gravity version of soccer might be played with larger, lighter balls and modified goals to accommodate species with limited mobility. This commitment to inclusivity ensures that the Galactic Games truly represent the entire galactic community.

Furthermore, the committee aims for a balance between individual and team-based sports. This allows participants to showcase both their individual prowess and their ability to collaborate within a team. Individual sports, such as the Psionic Duel, a mental chess match between two telepathic species, highlight individual skill and strategy. Team-based sports, like the Intergalactic Chase, a multi-species relay race through a complex obstacle course, emphasize teamwork and coordination. This balance ensures a diverse range of competitive experiences for participants and viewers alike.

Finally, the selected games must adhere to strict safety regulations. A comprehensive risk assessment is conducted for each sport, considering potential hazards and developing appropriate safety protocols. This includes establishing clear rules and regulations, providing necessary safety equipment, and training officials to enforce safety standards. The committee prioritizes the well-being of all participants, ensuring that the Galactic Games are conducted in a safe and responsible manner.

The selection of games for the Galactic Games is a complex and multifaceted process, requiring careful consideration of diversity, inclusivity, innovation, and safety. By embracing a democratic approach, fostering innovation, and prioritizing safety, the committee ensures that the Galactic Games become a truly unifying event, celebrating the rich tapestry of life across the galaxy. This careful curation of sports helps to foster interspecies understanding and promote a spirit of friendly competition throughout the cosmos.

3.2   Rule Modifications

Adapting established sports for interstellar competition presents unique challenges. Consider the Zydonian Whirlwind, a fast-paced game played on hovering platforms. Originally, players used their natural telekinetic abilities to manipulate the game orb. However, with the inclusion of species lacking such abilities, the rules must be modified. One solution involves providing specialized gloves that generate a controlled telekinetic field, leveling the playing field for all participants. This necessitates stringent testing of these gloves to ensure fairness and prevent any unintended advantages. Another approach could involve a redesign of the orb itself, embedding it with technology that responds to physical gestures or vocal commands, allowing species with diverse physical attributes to participate.

Rule modifications must also consider the physiological differences between species. The Gorthan Grapple, a test of strength and endurance, traditionally involves direct physical contact. For species with delicate exoskeletons or sensitive skin, such contact could be injurious. Introducing force-dampening fields around competitors allows for the sensation of grappling without the risk of physical harm. Alternatively, the competition could be restructured to focus on strategic positioning and manipulation of energy fields, retaining the core elements of the sport while ensuring participant safety. This shift would require careful re-calibration of scoring systems and the development of new judging criteria to accurately reflect skill and strategy.

Environmental considerations play a crucial role in rule adjustments. The Crystalline Comet Race, a thrilling race through asteroid fields, traditionally relies on the pilot's spatial awareness and reflexes. Introducing species with vastly different sensory perceptions requires a rethinking of the rules. For example, species that navigate primarily by sonar may require specialized equipment to translate sonar data into a visual representation of the asteroid field. Adjustments to the course layout itself might also be necessary. Adding beacons that emit species-specific sensory signals allows all participants to perceive the course effectively, preserving the challenge of the race while ensuring equal opportunity.

Furthermore, cultural sensitivities must be taken into account. The Nebulosian Dance of Deception, a game of strategic misdirection and illusion, traditionally involves elaborate costumes and intricate rituals. Some species may find certain costumes offensive or impractical. Adapting the rules to allow for species-specific attire while maintaining the spirit of deception is essential. This requires establishing clear guidelines on acceptable costume modifications while ensuring they do not provide a competitive advantage. Judges must be trained to recognize deceptive tactics across diverse cultural expressions, ensuring fair and unbiased assessments of performance.

The process of rule modification must be transparent and collaborative. A dedicated Rules Committee, composed of representatives from each participating species, should oversee the process. This committee should solicit feedback from athletes, coaches, and experts in each sport. Regularly scheduled meetings and open communication channels are crucial. This allows for thorough discussion and iterative refinement of proposed changes. Detailed documentation of all rule modifications, including rationale and potential impact on gameplay, should be maintained. This creates a clear record of the decision-making process and promotes accountability.

Testing and evaluation are vital. Prior to the official games, trial events should be held to test the modified rules in practice. These trial events offer valuable opportunities to identify unforeseen issues and gather feed-back from participants. Data collected during these trials should be an-alyzed to assess the impact of rule changes on gameplay, fairness, and safety. Based on this analysis, further adjustments can be made to ensure the rules are optimized for interstellar competition. This iterative process ensures the rules are robust and effectively address the unique challenges of interspecies sports.

Beyond the technical aspects, rule modifications should aim to preserve the core spirit and essence of each sport. While adaptations are necessary to accommodate diverse species, the fundamental skills, strategies, and challenges that define the sport should remain intact. This requires careful consideration of the impact of each rule change on the overall gameplay experience. Consulting with experts in the history and traditions of each sport can help ensure that modifications enhance inclusivity without com-promising the integrity of the game.

Finally, flexibility and adaptability are essential. The interstellar landscape is constantly evolving, with new species discovering the Galactic Games and bringing with them unique physical attributes and cultural perspec-tives. The rules governing interstellar sports must be dynamic and respon-sive to these changes. Establishing a clear process for ongoing review and revision of the rules ensures that the games remain inclusive, engaging, and relevant for all participants. This proactive approach fosters a sense of shared ownership and promotes the continued growth and evolution of interstellar sports.

3.3 Safety Protocols

The backbone of any successful interstellar sporting event lies in its meticulous approach to safety. This isn't just about preventing injuries, though that's paramount. It's about fostering an environment of trust and confidence for everyone involved, from athletes competing in zero-gravity to spectators arriving from nebulae light-years away. Consider this: you are responsible for the well-being of beings with vastly different physiologies, accustomed to varying gravitational pulls, atmospheric compositions, and even perceptions of reality. A comprehensive safety protocol is not a suggestion; it's the very fabric holding your event together.

Begin by meticulously assessing the risks inherent to each sport. Anti-gravity races, for instance, require different safety considerations than a game of cosmic chess. Analyze potential hazards: collisions, equipment malfunctions, exposure to extreme environments, or unexpected physiological reactions to a planet's unique conditions. This risk assessment should inform the development of sport-specific safety regulations. These regulations must be clearly communicated to all participants well in advance, translated into their respective languages, and presented in formats accessible to their sensory capabilities. Visual aids, interactive simulations, and even telepathic transmissions may be necessary.

Next, tailor your medical provisions to accommodate the diverse biological needs of interstellar athletes. Imagine a Gorthan with a triple-chambered heart suffering a cardiac event, or a Xylossian whose chitinous exoskeleton fractures during a high-impact collision. Your medical teams must be equipped to handle a spectrum of physiological anomalies. This necessitates specialized training, advanced medical technology capable of diagnosing and treating alien biology, and readily available antidotes to potential toxins or allergens present on the host planet. Moreover, establish designated medical facilities within the venue, easily accessible and equipped for rapid response to emergencies.

Spectator safety demands equal attention. Consider the potential for interspecies conflict due to cultural misunderstandings, differing social hierarchies, or even involuntary pheromonal responses. Implement crowd control strategies that respect diverse customs while maintaining order. Designate clear pathways for different species, considering their varying sizes, locomotion methods, and sensory sensitivities. Provide multilingual signage and real-time translation services to facilitate communication and prevent confusion. Ensure ample access to species-specific amenities, such as designated atmospheric zones, gravity regulators, and sustenance appropriate for their dietary requirements.

Beyond the immediate vicinity of the event, extend your safety protocols to encompass travel logistics. Interstellar journeys pose their own unique set of challenges. Collaborate with transportation providers to ensure vessels are equipped with appropriate life support systems and emergency protocols tailored to the diverse species onboard. Provide pre-departure briefings on safety procedures, including emergency evacuation drills and protocols for dealing with potential hazards like asteroid fields or solar flares.

Emergency preparedness is not a one-size-fits-all endeavor in the galactic arena. Develop contingency plans for a range of potential scenarios, from natural disasters to unforeseen technological malfunctions. Establish clear communication channels between event organizers, security personnel, medical teams, and local authorities on the host planet. Conduct regular safety drills to ensure a coordinated response in the event of an emergency. This includes evacuation procedures tailored to the venue's layout and the specific needs of the diverse attendees.

Furthermore, consider the psychological well-being of participants. The pressure of competing on an interstellar stage, coupled with the challenges of adapting to a foreign environment, can take a toll on athletes. Provide access to mental health professionals specializing in interspecies psychology. Offer counseling services and stress management techniques tailored to the unique cultural and psychological needs of each species.

Finally, the safety of your event hinges on effective communication. Establish a clear chain of command and ensure all personnel are thoroughly trained in their roles and responsibilities. Utilize advanced communication technologies to facilitate real-time information sharing between different teams and across language barriers. Regularly update safety protocols based on feedback from participants, spectators, and medical personnel. Continuously assess and refine your approach to safety, striving for a seamless and secure experience for everyone involved in this grand spectacle of interstellar sport. Remember, a successful event isn't just about the thrill of competition; it's about creating a safe and inclusive environment where the spirit of sportsmanship can truly flourish across the galaxy.

3.4 Dispute Resolution

Inevitably, even in the meticulously planned arena of interstellar sports, disagreements will arise. These can range from minor rule interpretations on the field to complex protests regarding eligibility or equipment malfunctions. A robust and impartial dispute resolution process is essential for maintaining the integrity of the Galactic Games and ensuring fair play for all participants. This process should be clearly defined and communicated to all teams and officials before the games commence. Transparency is key to building trust and acceptance of the outcomes.

The first step in any dispute resolution process involves a clear documentation of the incident. Designated officials, trained in observation and reporting, should be present at all events. These officials will record details of the disputed incident, including the time, location, involved parties, and a precise description of the events. Where possible, recordings from multiple angles should be captured to provide a comprehensive view of the situation. This documentation serves as the foundation upon which subsequent decisions are made. Think of it as creating an unimpeachable record, preserved for review.

Following the initial documentation, a preliminary review by an on-site adjudication panel is necessary. This panel, composed of experienced judges and sports officials, will examine the evidence gathered and hear initial statements from the involved parties. The goal of this preliminary review is to resolve the dispute quickly and efficiently, ideally before it escalates or disrupts the ongoing event. Minor infractions, such as technical fouls or procedural misunderstandings, can often be resolved at this stage. This quick action minimizes disruption and allows the games to proceed smoothly.

For more complex disputes, where the preliminary review cannot reach a satisfactory resolution, a formal appeal process must be available. This process involves submitting a written appeal to the Galactic Games Committee's Dispute Resolution Board. This board, composed of impartial experts from diverse galactic backgrounds, provides a neutral platform for thorough investigation and deliberation. The board will review all available evidence, including witness testimonies, expert analysis, and any relevant regulations. Their decisions will be binding and final, ensuring a consistent application of rules and regulations across all events.

The Dispute Resolution Board will operate under a strict code of conduct and follow established procedures to guarantee fairness and impartiality. All parties involved in a dispute will be given equal opportunity to present their case and challenge evidence presented against them. This includes the right to legal representation, provided the representative adheres to the Galactic Games Committee's regulations. Transparency in the process is paramount, and all decisions, along with their justifications, will be made publicly available after the conclusion of the proceedings. This open approach fosters trust in the system and reinforces the commitment to fair play.

Furthermore, to ensure the efficacy and adaptability of the dispute resolution process, a continuous review and improvement mechanism is crucial. Following the conclusion of the Galactic Games, the Dispute Resolution Board will conduct a thorough analysis of all disputes handled. This analysis will identify any trends, patterns, or recurring issues that might indicate weaknesses in the existing rules or procedures. Recommendations for improvements will be submitted to the Galactic Games Committee for consideration and implementation in future events. This continuous improvement cycle ensures that the dispute resolution process remains effective, fair, and adaptable to the ever-evolving landscape of interstellar sports.

Finally, it is essential to address the issue of cultural sensitivity within the dispute resolution framework. The vast diversity of species participating in the Galactic Games necessitates a nuanced approach to conflict resolution. Cultural differences in communication styles, perceptions of fairness, and methods of expressing disagreement must be acknowledged and respected. The Dispute Resolution Board will receive comprehensive training on intercultural communication and conflict resolution to ensure that all participants feel heard and understood. Interpreters and cultural advisors will be readily available to facilitate communication and bridge any cultural gaps that may arise during the proceedings. By incorporating cultural sensitivity into every stage of the dispute resolution process, the Galactic Games Committee strives to create an environment where all participants feel valued and respected, regardless of their planetary origin. This commitment to inclusivity reinforces the spirit of unity and sportsmanship that lies at the heart of the Galactic Games.

3.5 Doping Control

The cornerstone of fair competition in the Galactic Games rests upon robust doping control. Maintaining the integrity of interstellar sport demands a comprehensive and nuanced approach, recognizing the physiological diversity of participating species and the ever-evolving landscape of performance-enhancing substances and techniques. This chapter will delve into the intricate procedures and considerations necessary for effective doping control, ensuring a level playing field for all athletes.

Establishing clear and universally understood regulations is paramount. The Galactic Games Committee must publish a comprehensive list of prohibited substances and methods, categorized by their physiological effects and potential for performance enhancement. This list must be readily accessible to all participants, translated into relevant galactic languages, and regularly updated to reflect advancements in bio-enhancement technology. Consideration should be given to species-specific metabolic processes and the potential for naturally occurring compounds in one species to provide an unfair advantage to another. For example, the Xylos' natural bioluminescence might be considered a performance enhancer in low-light competitions, requiring careful regulation. Regular review and consultation with experts from various species are essential to maintain the relevance and fairness of these regulations.

Implementing a rigorous testing program is crucial for enforcing these regulations. Testing should be conducted both in-competition and out-of-competition, with a focus on random selection and targeted testing based on intelligence and performance analysis. Sample collection procedures must be standardized across species, accounting for physiological differences in excretion and metabolism. Chain-of-custody protocols must be meticulously followed to ensure the integrity and traceability of samples from collection to analysis. This involves secure storage, transport, and handling of samples, minimizing the risk of contamination or tampering. Dedicated, trained personnel from each participating species should oversee sample collection from their own athletes, respecting cultural sensitivities and ensuring proper protocol adherence.

Furthermore, the analysis of collected samples requires sophisticated laboratories equipped to handle the unique biological makeup of diverse species. These laboratories should be accredited by the Galactic Games Committee and adhere to stringent quality control standards. Analysis methods must be validated for accuracy and sensitivity, capable of detecting a wide range of prohibited substances and metabolites. Given the vast distances involved in interstellar travel, consideration should be given to establishing regional testing facilities to expedite sample processing and minimize logistical challenges. Collaboration with leading scientific institutions across the galaxy will be essential in developing and validating these advanced analytical techniques.

Educating athletes on the dangers of doping and promoting a culture of clean sport is just as important as detection and enforcement. The Galactic Games Committee should develop comprehensive educational programs that are tailored to different species, cultural backgrounds, and sporting disciplines. These programs should cover the health risks associated with performance-enhancing substances, the ethical implications of doping, and the consequences of violating anti-doping regulations. Interactive workshops, online resources, and mentorship programs can be utilized to disseminate information and foster a sense of shared responsibility in maintaining the integrity of the Games. Highlighting the stories of athletes who have chosen the path of clean competition can serve as powerful inspiration and reinforce the values of fair play and sportsmanship.

Managing therapeutic use exemptions (TUEs) is another critical aspect of doping control. Athletes with legitimate medical conditions may require medications that are otherwise prohibited under the regulations. A transparent and standardized process for applying for and granting TUEs is essential. A panel of independent medical experts from diverse species should review each application, ensuring that the medication is necessary for the athlete's health and does not confer an unfair competitive advantage. Confidentiality and data protection protocols must be strictly adhered to throughout the TUE process.

Addressing potential challenges unique to interstellar competition is paramount. The vast distances and varied environments can impact athlete physiology and complicate doping control procedures. Factors such as interstellar travel, gravitational variations, and exposure to different atmospheric conditions can influence metabolism and excretion rates of prohibited substances. Research and development in adapting doping control protocols to these unique circumstances is crucial for maintaining the effectiveness of the program. Furthermore, cultural variations in attitudes towards performance enhancement may necessitate tailored educational and outreach programs to ensure universal understanding and compliance.

Finally, a robust appeals process must be in place for athletes who are charged with anti-doping rule violations. This process should guarantee due process, fairness, and impartiality. Athletes should have the right to present their case before an independent panel, with access to legal representation and expert testimony. Decisions made by the appeals panel must be based on scientific evidence and the established anti-doping regulations. Transparency and accountability in the appeals process are essential for maintaining the credibility of the doping control program and ensuring the fairness of the Galactic Games. The committee must also establish clear sanctions for violations, ranging from warnings and fines to disqualifications and bans, proportionate to the severity of the offense and any previous violations. This comprehensive approach to doping control is not just a set of rules, but a commitment to preserving the spirit of competition and celebrating the athletic achievements of all participants in the Galactic Games.

4 Chapter 4: Participant Management

The cornerstone of any successful interstellar sporting event lies in the seamless management of its participants. This involves a multifaceted approach that begins long before the opening ceremony and extends well beyond the final whistle. Foremost among these responsibilities is the establishment of a clear and efficient team registration process. This process must be accessible galaxy-wide, catering to the diverse technological capabilities of different civilizations. A dedicated online portal, translated into commonly used galactic languages, should be the central hub for registration. This portal should clearly outline eligibility criteria, including species-specific physical requirements and any restrictions based on previous competitive history. Teams should be required to submit all necessary documentation, such as player rosters, waivers, and proof of insurance, through this secure platform. Automated confirmation systems can streamline communication and minimize manual processing.

Beyond registration, consider the monumental task of coordinating interstellar travel for hundreds, potentially thousands, of participants. The

Galactic Games Committee must establish partnerships with reputable interstellar transport providers. Negotiating discounted rates for bulk travel, and securing transport vessels equipped to handle the unique physiological needs of various species, are crucial. This could involve specialized atmospheric controls, gravity adjustments, and dietary provisions. Travel itineraries should be carefully planned and communicated to teams, taking into account potential delays due to wormhole instability or unexpected celestial events. Arrival and departure schedules need to be synchronized with venue availability and practice session allotments.

Accommodation presents another layer of complexity. The Games Committee must secure lodging that caters to the diverse needs of participating species. This goes beyond simply providing suitable sleeping arrangements. Consider the dietary needs of silicon-based life forms, the temperature requirements of cryophilic athletes, or the specific atmospheric pressures needed by participants from high-gravity planets. Dedicated cultural liaisons can assist teams in navigating unfamiliar customs and planetary regulations. Pre-event cultural sensitivity training for both participants and local populations can foster understanding and promote a welcoming atmosphere. Providing access to specialized equipment, like gravity simulators or atmospheric regulators, within the accommodation facilities can further enhance the comfort and well-being of participants.

The logistics of participant management extend to the competition arena itself. Designated team areas within the venue should be equipped with species-specific amenities, such as hydration stations dispensing various liquids and gases, and temperature-controlled rest areas. Real-time translation services are essential for effective communication between officials, athletes, and coaching staff from different linguistic backgrounds. Clear signage and wayfinding systems, utilizing both visual and olfactory cues for species that rely on scent-based navigation, should be implemented throughout the venue.

Medical support for participants is another critical consideration. A team of medical professionals specializing in xenobiology and interspecies physiology should be readily available. Medical facilities must be equipped to handle a wide range of medical emergencies, from treating radiation sickness in energy-based life forms to repairing the exoskeletons of insectoid athletes. Pre-event medical screenings, tailored to the unique physiology of each species, can help identify potential health risks and prevent complications during competition.

Beyond the physical needs, the psychological well-being of participants should be a priority. The Games Committee should provide access to mental health professionals experienced in interspecies psychology. These professionals can assist athletes in coping with the stress of competition, cultural adjustment challenges, and homesickness. Organized social events and cultural exchange programs can further foster camaraderie and create a sense of community among participants from different worlds. Dedicated spaces for meditation and spiritual practices, catering to a wide range of beliefs and customs, can provide a sanctuary for athletes seeking solace and mental clarity.

Managing participant nutrition is a complex undertaking, given the diverse dietary requirements of interstellar athletes. The Games Committee must work closely with culinary experts specializing in xenogastronome to develop menus that meet the nutritional needs of all participants. This involves sourcing ingredients from across the galaxy and preparing meals that adhere to species-specific dietary restrictions. Dedicated dining areas, equipped with appropriate atmospheric controls and specialized utensils, should be provided within the venue. Food safety protocols must be rigorously enforced to prevent cross-contamination and allergic reactions.

Finally, participant management includes ensuring a smooth departure process. This involves coordinating transportation to departure points, processing any necessary customs documentation, and providing assistance with baggage handling. Post-event surveys can gather valuable feedback from participants, helping the Games Committee identify areas for improvement in future events. This continuous improvement process ensures the Galactic Games remain a premier showcase of interstellar athleticism and intercultural exchange. By prioritizing the well-being and comfort of its participants, the Games Committee fosters an environment conducive to fair play, sportsmanship, and the celebration of athletic excellence on a galactic scale.

4.1 Team Registration

The cornerstone of any successful interstellar sporting event lies in the meticulous management of participating teams. This involves a comprehensive registration process that ensures all teams are properly documented, eligible, and prepared for the Galactic Games. This process, while complex, can be streamlined through a structured approach, beginning with the dissemination of clear guidelines to all prospective participants. These guidelines, available via a dedicated Galactic Games network portal, will detail every step, from initial application to final confirmation.

Teams must first declare their intention to participate by submitting a preliminary application form. This form will collect basic information such as the team's name, planet of origin, the sport they wish to compete in, and a preliminary roster of team members. This initial step allows the committee to gauge the level of interest and begin allocating resources accordingly. Crucially, it also triggers the next phase: verification of eligibility.

Eligibility criteria, while varying slightly depending on the specific sport, generally revolve around a few key factors. Teams must demonstrate that they are officially recognized by their planet's governing body for the chosen sport. Proof of participation in qualifying events, where applicable, must also be submitted. Individual athletes will be screened against a galactic database to ensure compliance with regulations regarding past disciplinary actions or doping violations. This rigorous verification process ensures a fair and competitive environment for all participants.

Upon successful verification of eligibility, teams are then required to submit a comprehensive registration package. This package encompasses detailed information about each team member, including biometric data, medical history, and emergency contact information. It also includes waivers and liability forms, crucial for navigating the complexities of interstellar legal frameworks. Furthermore, each team must submit proof of insurance that covers interstellar travel, competition-related injuries, and potential liability claims. This meticulous documentation ensures the safety and well-being of all participants, mitigating potential risks and complications.

Managing the influx of registration packages requires a sophisticated, automated system. Upon submission, each package is digitally processed and cross-referenced against the established criteria. Any discrepancies or missing information are flagged, and the respective team is notified immediately through the Galactic Games network. This real-time communication minimizes delays and ensures a smooth, efficient process.

A dedicated team within the Galactic Games Committee is responsible for overseeing the entire registration process. They provide support to participating teams, answer queries, and resolve any issues that may arise. This dedicated support team ensures that all teams, regardless of their planet of origin or technological capabilities, have equal access to the information and assistance they need. This commitment to inclusivity and accessibility is paramount to the success of the Galactic Games.

The final stage of team registration involves the issuance of official participation credentials. These credentials, encrypted with advanced security protocols, serve as identification and grant access to various facilities and services throughout the Games. They also allow teams to officially participate in training sessions, scheduled scrimmages, and ultimately, the competitive events themselves. This formalized system ensures that only authorized individuals are permitted access to restricted areas, maintaining the integrity and security of the Games.

Furthermore, the registration process feeds directly into the logistics planning for the event. Knowing the exact number of participants from each planet allows for efficient allocation of resources, including accommodation, transportation, and catering. This integration streamlines the overall event management and ensures a seamless experience for all participants. The efficient management of team registration is an integral part of organizing a successful interstellar sporting event. By implementing a structured approach, leveraging technology, and providing dedicated support, the Galactic Games Committee can ensure a smooth and efficient process for all participating teams. This, in turn, sets the stage for a truly spectacular and memorable event, celebrating the spirit of competition and unity across the galaxy. Beyond the logistical aspects, successful team registration lays the foundation for fair play, athlete safety, and ultimately, the successful execution of the Games themselves. It is the first step towards ensuring that the Galactic Games are not just a competition, but a celebration of interstellar camaraderie and sporting excellence.

4.2 Travel Logistics

Coordinating the arrival and departure of athletes, support staff, and dignitaries from potentially thousands of star systems presents a unique logistical challenge. This chapter will dissect the complexities of interstellar travel management for the Galactic Games, ensuring a seamless and efficient process for all participants. First, we'll establish a comprehensive travel registration system. This system, accessible via a secure galactic network portal, will collect vital information: species-specific needs, preferred modes of transport, dietary restrictions, and any necessary quarantine protocols. This centralized database will streamline communication and allow us to anticipate and address individual requirements efficiently. Think of it as a galactic airport hub, but handling far more complex variables than simple luggage.

Next, we delve into the intricacies of interstellar transportation. Participants may arrive via a variety of methods: generation ships, hyperspace-capable vessels, wormhole transit, or even teleportation, depending on their technological advancement. We must establish designated arrival and departure zones for each transport type, ensuring efficient traffic flow and minimizing disruption to the host planet. These zones will be equipped with specialized docking facilities and customs protocols tailored to the specific requirements of different species and technologies. Imagine the controlled chaos of a spaceport bustling with beings from all corners of the galaxy.

Accommodation presents another layer of complexity. Participants will require habitats that cater to their specific physiological needs. This goes beyond simply providing oxygen or adjusting gravity. Considerations must include atmospheric pressure, ambient radiation levels, temperature, and even the availability of specific nutrients or energy sources. Constructing modular, adaptable habitats that can be quickly configured to meet these varied requirements will be essential. Picture a city built overnight, morphing and adapting to house a kaleidoscope of life forms.

Cultural adaptation and support are crucial for a positive participant experience. Many athletes and officials will be visiting a new planetary system for the first time, encountering unfamiliar customs, languages, and social norms. Providing cultural orientation programs, multilingual support staff, and access to translation technology will help mitigate potential culture shock and foster understanding among diverse participants. This is about creating a welcoming atmosphere where everyone feels respected and valued, regardless of their origin.

Beyond the athletes themselves, consider the logistical needs of their accompanying equipment. Some sports may require specialized gear, ranging from zero-gravity training apparatuses to genetically modified sporting animals. Transporting and storing this equipment safely and efficiently demands careful planning. Dedicated cargo bays, specialized containment fields, and climate-controlled storage facilities will be necessary to preserve the integrity of this diverse range of equipment. Think of a highly organized intergalactic warehouse, filled with everything from hoverboards to sentient energy spheres.

Medical considerations are paramount. Interstellar travel can be taxing, even with advanced technology. Providing on-site medical facilities equipped to handle a wide range of species-specific ailments and injuries is essential. This includes having access to universal translators, bio-regenerative technology, and medical personnel trained in xenobiology. We must ensure prompt and effective medical care for all participants, safeguarding their health and well-being throughout the Games. Visualize a state-of-the-art medical center, capable of treating anything from a broken bone to a dislocated phase-shifted appendage.

Managing the flow of information is also vital. Real-time updates on arrival and departure schedules, transportation changes, accommodation assignments, and event-related announcements must be readily available to all participants. A dedicated communication network, accessible through personal devices or holographic displays, will ensure everyone stays informed and connected. This is like a personalized galactic news feed, keeping participants constantly updated on everything they need to know.

Finally, contingency planning is crucial. Unexpected events, from solar flares to political upheavals, can disrupt travel plans. Establishing backup transportation routes, emergency accommodation facilities, and flexible scheduling protocols will allow us to adapt quickly and minimize disruption in the face of unforeseen circumstances. This is about having a plan B, C, and even D in place to ensure the Games proceed smoothly no matter what challenges arise. Successfully managing the travel logistics of the Galactic Games requires meticulous planning, advanced technology, and a deep understanding of the diverse needs of interstellar participants. By prioritizing efficiency, communication, and cultural sensitivity, we can create a positive and memorable experience for everyone involved, ensuring the Games become a true celebration of galactic unity and sporting excellence. Consider the magnitude of orchestrating the arrival and departure of an entire civilization's worth of athletes. That's the scale of the operation we are undertaking.

5 Chapter 5: Broadcasting & Media

Negotiating broadcast rights for interstellar events presents unique complexities. Consider the sheer scale: transmissions must traverse vast distances, often requiring relay stations and specialized technology to penetrate nebular clouds or bypass gravitational distortions. Agreements must account for varying technological standards and communication protocols across different galactic civilizations. Rights should be segmented strategically, offering packages for specific sports, highlight reels, or even exclusive behind-the-scenes access. Think tiered access for different media outlets, from planetary news networks to galaxy-wide entertainment conglomerates. This tiered approach maximizes revenue while ensuring broad coverage across diverse audiences.

Interstellar broadcasting demands more than just adapting terrestrial systems. Consider the temporal discrepancies inherent in interstellar communication. Live broadcasts might be impractical for events occurring light-years away. Delayed broadcasts, carefully edited to accommodate different species' perception of time, become necessary. Subtitling and translation for a multitude of languages, some potentially non-verbal, pose another challenge. Invest in advanced AI-powered translation software capable of real-time interpretation and culturally sensitive adaptation, ensuring accurate and engaging commentary for all viewers. Exploring holographic projection technology allows spectators to experience the event as if they were present, adding another dimension to viewership and potentially generating additional revenue streams.

Effective press relations necessitate understanding diverse galactic cultures and media landscapes. Journalists from different species have varying customs, ethical guidelines, and reporting styles. Establish a clear press accreditation system, providing detailed information about the event, participating species, and relevant regulations. Designate dedicated press areas equipped with translation devices and species-specific amenities. Organize pre-event briefings and post-event interviews with athletes and officials. Tailor press releases for different planetary media outlets, highlighting aspects relevant to their respective audiences. Fostering positive relationships with galactic media representatives can significantly boost the event's profile and ensure favorable coverage.

Social media in the galactic context presents a vast and complex network. Platforms vary drastically across civilizations, utilizing diverse communication technologies and social structures. Understanding the dominant social media platforms within target demographics is crucial for effective outreach. Engage influencers within different species to promote the event and generate excitement within their respective communities. Create interactive content, polls, and virtual reality experiences to engage audiences on their preferred platforms. Monitor social media sentiment to gauge public opinion and address any concerns promptly. A well-executed social media strategy can significantly expand the event's reach and build a dedicated fan base across the galaxy.

Developing a comprehensive marketing strategy requires a multifaceted approach. Consider merchandise, ranging from species-specific apparel to holographic collectibles. Offer exclusive virtual reality experiences, allowing fans to participate in simulated games or interact with their favorite athletes. Partner with galactic corporations to sponsor events and create themed promotions. Organize pre-event festivities on different planets to generate local excitement and encourage attendance. Develop a consistent brand identity that resonates across different cultures and species, using universally understood symbols and imagery. A well-crafted marketing strategy creates revenue streams beyond broadcasting rights, solidifying the event's financial stability and long-term viability.

Think about dedicated broadcasting crews trained in intercultural communication. These specialists must understand not only language translation but also subtle nuances in body language, customs, and humor. Equipping them with advanced communication technology ensures accurate and sensitive reporting while minimizing potential cultural misunderstandings. Develop partnerships with established galactic media outlets to leverage their existing infrastructure and audience reach. These collaborations offer valuable resources and expertise, streamlining the broadcasting process while maximizing viewership. Offering exclusive content and behind-the-scenes access incentivizes media partners to invest in the event's promotion.

Promoting inclusivity in broadcasting requires careful consideration of accessibility. Develop adaptive technologies for viewers with sensory limitations, ensuring everyone can experience the thrill of interstellar sports. Offer commentary in various formats, including visual and tactile interpretations for non-audio-reliant species. Ensure that venues are equipped with accessibility features for spectators with physical disabilities, further promoting inclusivity and demonstrating a commitment to providing a welcoming environment for all. These measures demonstrate a commitment to accessibility and broaden the event's reach, fostering goodwill among diverse galactic communities.

Navigating legal frameworks across different planetary systems requires a dedicated legal team. These experts must be versed in interstellar law and familiar with the regulations of participating species' home planets. They are responsible for drafting contracts that comply with all relevant legal systems, protecting the event organizers from potential liabilities and ensuring compliance with broadcasting standards. Their expertise is crucial in resolving disputes and navigating the complexities of interstellar intellectual property rights, ensuring a smooth and legally sound operation.

Managing media inquiries from across the galaxy can be overwhelming. Establish a dedicated media relations team responsible for fielding inquiries, scheduling interviews, and disseminating information to the galactic press. This team acts as a central point of contact, ensuring consistent messaging and efficient communication with diverse media outlets. Providing accurate and timely responses fosters positive relationships with journalists and ensures consistent coverage of the event, enhancing public perception and promoting transparency. Consider offering media training to athletes and officials, preparing them for interactions with galactic media and ensuring they can effectively represent the event. Leveraging emerging technologies can enhance the broadcasting experience. Explore the use of augmented reality to overlay statistics, player profiles, and real-time analysis onto the broadcast feed, adding another layer of engagement for viewers. Invest in interactive virtual reality experiences that allow fans to virtually attend the games, explore the venues, and even interact with athletes, creating unique and immersive experiences that generate additional revenue streams. These innovations enhance audience engagement and offer unique viewing opportunities, further solidifying the event's position as a cutting-edge spectacle.

5.1 Rights & Licensing

Navigating the complex landscape of interstellar broadcasting rights requires a meticulous and strategic approach. Consider the vastness of the galaxy: different sectors, varying levels of technological advancement, diverse species with unique communication methods. A comprehensive plan is crucial for maximizing reach and revenue while respecting intellectual property and cultural sensitivities. Begin by establishing clear ownership of the broadcasting rights for the Galactic Games. This involves documenting all aspects of the event, from the opening ceremony to individual competitions, ensuring a solid legal foundation for any future negotiations.

With ownership established, the next step involves segmenting the galactic market. Divide the galaxy into broadcasting zones based on technological capabilities, preferred media formats, and cultural relevance of the Games. This segmentation allows for tailored licensing agreements that cater to specific audiences, maximizing both viewership and revenue potential. For instance, a sector heavily reliant on holographic projections would require a different broadcasting package compared to one that primarily uses neural interfaces.

Within each broadcasting zone, identify potential partners. Look for established interstellar media networks, specialized sports broadcasters, and emerging platforms with a strong presence in their respective sectors. Research their audience demographics, broadcasting capabilities, and reputation for fair dealing. Directly contacting these potential partners allows for personalized negotiations and mutually beneficial agreements. This tailored approach fosters stronger relationships and increases the likelihood of successful long-term partnerships.

Crafting the licensing agreements themselves requires careful consideration. Each agreement should clearly define the scope of the rights granted, the duration of the license, the territories covered, and the financial terms. Specify the permitted uses of the broadcast footage, including live broadcasts, delayed broadcasts, highlights reels, and archival footage. Incorporate provisions for language localization, subtitling, and commentary tailored to the specific cultural context of each broadcasting zone. This level of detail ensures that the Games are accessible and engaging to a diverse galactic audience.

Beyond the technical aspects, consider the cultural implications. Some species may have strict customs regarding the depiction of athletic competition, while others might have specific sensitivities around commercialization. Consulting with cultural experts from each sector can help navigate these complexities and avoid unintended offense. Building these relationships not only ensures respectful broadcasting practices but also fosters goodwill and strengthens the Galactic Games' reputation throughout the galaxy.

Moreover, factor in the technological disparities across different sectors. Some regions may still rely on older broadcasting technologies, requiring specific adaptations and potentially separate licensing agreements. Offering different tiers of broadcasting packages based on technological capabilities ensures broader accessibility while maximizing revenue generation across the diverse galactic market. This tiered approach caters to a wider audience and promotes inclusivity in the Galactic Games.

Revenue models for licensing agreements can vary. Consider traditional models such as upfront fees, revenue sharing, and per-view charges. Explore innovative approaches such as tiered access based on content, interactive features, and virtual reality experiences. The chosen model should align with the specific market dynamics of each broadcasting zone and the overall financial goals of the Galactic Games. Experimenting with different revenue models can unlock new streams of income and enhance the financial sustainability of the event.

Monitoring compliance with licensing agreements is critical. Implement tracking mechanisms to ensure that broadcasters adhere to the agreed-upon terms, including the scope of usage, territorial restrictions, and payment schedules. Regular audits and transparent reporting procedures maintain the integrity of the licensing agreements and protect the intellectual property of the Galactic Games. This diligence safeguards the Games' financial interests and prevents unauthorized exploitation of the broadcast content.

Anticipate potential disputes and incorporate clear dispute resolution mechanisms into the licensing agreements. Specify the preferred method of resolution, whether it be mediation, arbitration, or recourse to a designated interstellar court. Clearly defining these procedures upfront minimizes disruptions and ensures swift and equitable resolution of any disagreements that may arise. This proactive approach fosters a positive working relationship with broadcasters and maintains the smooth operation of the Galactic Games.

Finally, maintain open communication with all licensing partners throughout the event. Regularly provide updates on scheduling changes, athlete profiles, and key storylines to enhance their broadcasting efforts. This collaborative approach strengthens relationships, ensures accurate and engaging coverage, and maximizes the reach of the Galactic Games across the galaxy. By working together, the Galactic Games Committee and its broadcasting partners can create a truly spectacular and memorable event for audiences throughout the galaxy. This collective effort will solidify the Games' legacy as a premier interstellar sporting event.

5.2 Interstellar Broadcast

Broadcasting interstellar sporting events presents unique challenges unseen in any terrestrial equivalent. Consider the sheer scale: signals must traverse light-years to reach audiences scattered across diverse star systems. This chapter delves into the complexities of transmitting these events, ensuring a captivating experience for viewers regardless of their location in the galaxy. We'll examine the technical hurdles, the strategies for overcoming them, and the intricacies of managing a galactic-scale broadcast operation.

First, consider signal degradation. Traveling across such vast distances, even tightly focused transmissions weaken and disperse. Relay stations strategically positioned throughout the galaxy become crucial, boosting and redirecting the signal to maintain integrity. These stations must be precisely calibrated to account for the subtle gravitational lensing effects of celestial bodies along the transmission path, ensuring minimal distortion. Redundant systems are a necessity, safeguarding against unforeseen outages or technical malfunctions at any point in the relay network. Testing protocols must be rigorously implemented to guarantee signal strength and clarity at the receiving end.

Then, there's the issue of real-time versus delayed broadcasts. Given the limitations of faster-than-light communication, achieving true real-time across the galaxy remains impractical. Spectators on distant planets might experience delays ranging from minutes to days, depending on their location relative to the event. Strategies for managing these delays include tailored broadcast schedules for different sectors, interactive replay features, and pre-event analysis segments to bridge the temporal gap. This necessitates a complex scheduling system, carefully coordinating transmissions to minimize disruption and maximize viewer engagement.

Encoding and decoding the signal for diverse species presents another layer of complexity. Visual and auditory perception varies dramatically across galactic civilizations. Some species perceive light frequencies outside the human visible spectrum, while others rely on entirely different sensory modalities. A universal broadcast must be adaptable, seamlessly translating the event into a format comprehensible to each species. This involves advanced encoding techniques that incorporate multiple data streams, allowing receivers to decode the signal based on their specific physiological requirements. Pre-event consultations with representatives from participating species are essential to ensure compatibility and optimize the viewing experience.

Beyond the technical aspects, managing the broadcast team poses its own set of logistical challenges. Coordinating a team dispersed across the galaxy requires meticulous planning and robust communication channels.

Team members must be fluent in multiple galactic languages and possess a deep understanding of the nuances of interstellar communication protocols. Regular training sessions and simulations are essential to maintain proficiency and prepare the team for the unpredictable nature of live interstellar broadcasts. Furthermore, establishing clear lines of command and communication hierarchies is crucial for efficient decision-making and rapid response to unforeseen technical difficulties.

Furthermore, the sheer volume of data generated by an interstellar sporting event is staggering. Multiple camera angles, sensor data, and commentary feeds contribute to a massive data stream that must be efficiently managed and transmitted. This requires advanced compression algorithms and robust data handling systems to avoid bottlenecks and ensure seamless transmission. The development of dedicated interstellar broadcast protocols becomes essential to manage this data deluge effectively. Such protocols must incorporate error correction mechanisms and data redundancy to safeguard against data loss or corruption during transmission.

Audience engagement and interactivity are also crucial considerations. Implementing real-time polling and interactive features allows viewers to participate in the event, enhancing their immersion and fostering a sense of community across vast interstellar distances. However, managing this level of interactivity requires sophisticated data processing capabilities and robust server infrastructure. The development of specialized software platforms capable of handling the demands of galactic-scale interactive broadcasting becomes a necessity.

Monetizing the broadcast without alienating audiences represents another significant challenge. Traditional advertising models may not translate effectively to an interstellar context. Exploring alternative revenue streams, such as subscription-based access or micro-transactions for exclusive content, could prove more viable. Careful consideration must be given to the cultural sensitivities and economic realities of diverse galactic civilizations to ensure a sustainable and equitable broadcast model. Market research across various sectors of the galaxy becomes crucial for informing these decisions.

Finally, legal and ethical considerations surrounding interstellar broadcasting must be addressed. Issues of intellectual property, broadcast rights, and censorship vary significantly across different star systems. Establishing a universal framework for managing these issues is paramount. This requires extensive collaboration and negotiation between participating civilizations to ensure a fair and legally sound broadcast operation. The formation of an interstellar broadcasting regulatory body could prove invaluable in navigating this complex legal landscape. This body would be responsible for establishing standards, mediating disputes, and ensuring compliance with established regulations. Its composition should reflect the diversity of the galactic community, incorporating representatives from various star systems and legal traditions. This collaborative approach fosters trust and promotes a harmonious broadcasting environment across the galaxy.

5.3   Press Relations

Effective press relations are crucial for the success of any interstellar sporting event. Cultivating positive relationships with media outlets across the galaxy will ensure widespread coverage and generate excitement for the Games. This involves a multi-faceted approach encompassing pre-event outreach, on-site facilitation, and post-event follow-up. Remember, the galactic press corps represents a diverse range of species with varying communication protocols and cultural nuances.

Begin by compiling a comprehensive media database. This database should categorize media outlets by sector, species, preferred communication methods (e.g., holographic transmission, subspace relay), and areas of interest. Understanding the specific needs of each media outlet allows for targeted outreach and personalized communication. Provide them with detailed information packets about the Games, including schedules, athlete profiles, venue details, and historical context. Consider offering exclusive interviews with key figures like committee members, prominent athletes, and even sports historians who can provide expert commentary.

Develop a dedicated press center at the event venue. Equip this space with advanced communication technology to accommodate various species' communication needs. Provide translators, both biological and technological, to ensure seamless information flow. Ensure the press center offers comfortable workspaces, ample power sources for their equipment, and readily accessible catering facilities. Real-time data feeds of event results, athlete statistics, and high-resolution images should be readily available for download and dissemination. Designate a press liaison team specifically trained to handle inquiries, facilitate interviews, and address any media-related concerns promptly and professionally. This team should be well-versed in intercultural communication and conflict resolution.

Organize press conferences strategically throughout the Games. These provide an opportunity to highlight significant moments, address controversial issues, and offer expert analysis of sporting events. Invite athletes and coaches to share their experiences and perspectives. Provide multilingual transcripts and holographic recordings of the press conferences to ensure accessibility for media outlets unable to attend in person. Consider hosting smaller, more intimate media roundtables with specific journalists to foster stronger relationships and provide in-depth background information on particular sports or athletes.

Cultivate relationships with prominent galactic sports journalists and influencers. Offer them exclusive access to behind-the-scenes events, training sessions, and athlete interviews. These individuals hold significant sway over public opinion and can significantly impact the Games' perception throughout the galaxy. Provide them with accurate and timely information, respecting their journalistic integrity while fostering open communication. Encourage them to experience the cultural exchange aspects of the Games, fostering a deeper appreciation for the diverse species participating.

Prepare press releases for major events, including opening and closing ceremonies, record-breaking performances, and any unexpected occurrences. Distribute these releases promptly through various channels, including direct transmission to media outlets, official Games website postings, and social media platforms. Ensure that press releases are concise, accurate, and engaging, providing all necessary information while respecting journalistic deadlines. Include high-quality images and video footage whenever possible to enhance the storytelling and visual appeal of the releases. Post-event, send thank-you messages to all participating media outlets. Offer them access to a comprehensive archive of event footage, photographs, and official documents. Conduct a post-event media survey to gather feedback on their experience and identify areas for improvement in future Games. Continue cultivating relationships with key media contacts, keeping them informed about future plans and inviting them to participate in upcoming events. Building long-term relationships with the galactic press is an ongoing process that will pay dividends in future iterations of the Games.

Leverage digital platforms to share highlights, interviews, and behind-the-scenes glimpses of the Games. Encourage fan interaction and create engaging content that resonates with a diverse galactic audience. Implement a robust social media strategy encompassing multiple platforms. Assign dedicated social media managers fluent in various intergalactic languages and cultural nuances. Monitor social media channels for real-time feedback, addressing concerns and engaging with fans directly. Encourage athletes and teams to share their experiences on their own social media platforms, amplifying the reach of the Games and fostering a sense of community.

Understanding the importance of cultural sensitivity in press relations is paramount. Different species have different communication styles, customs, and expectations. Thorough research and preparation will enable you to navigate these complexities effectively. Employing cultural advisors and sensitivity trainers for the press liaison team can prove invaluable. Providing culturally appropriate catering, respecting personal space boundaries, and using correct forms of address will demonstrate respect for the diverse media representatives attending the Games.

Remember, effective press relations are a cornerstone of a successful interstellar sporting event. By building strong relationships with the galactic press, facilitating their work, and providing them with timely and accurate information, you can ensure that the Games receive the widespread coverage and positive publicity they deserve. This, in turn, will elevate the profile of the event, attract sponsors, and generate excitement among fans throughout the galaxy.

5.4   Social Media

Harnessing the immense power of social media is crucial for the success of the Galactic Games. This involves not just broadcasting information but cultivating a vibrant online community around the event. Think of it as building excitement, not simply advertising. Consider species-specific platforms and communication preferences. Some species might favor visual platforms, others audio-based, while some might rely on telepathic networks entirely. Adapting your strategy to these nuances is key to maximizing engagement. Translate crucial information into commonly understood galactic languages. Ensure your team understands the cultural sensitivities of different species when crafting messages. A seemingly innocuous message on one platform could be considered offensive on another.

Engagement is paramount. Don't just broadcast; interact. Run polls asking fans to predict winners or vote on their favorite athlete. Host Q&A sessions with prominent athletes. Create interactive games related to the sports being played. Encourage user-generated content by launching contests for fan art, cheers, or even short stories about the Games. Consider implementing a system where fans earn points for interacting with your social media content. These points could be redeemed for exclusive digital merchandise, early access to ticket sales, or even a chance to meet their favorite athletes. This fosters a sense of ownership and encourages continuous participation.

Live-streaming behind-the-scenes glimpses into athlete training, venue preparations, and the cultural exchange happening between different species at the Games. This provides an exclusive look into the event beyond the competitions, adding another layer of engagement. Create dedicated hashtags for each sport, team, and even individual athletes. This allows fans to easily follow their interests and join conversations with like-minded individuals. Monitor these hashtags to identify trending topics and engage in relevant discussions, demonstrating that the Games committee is actively listening to its audience.

Partner with influential figures within different galactic communities. These could be famous athletes, respected scientists, or even popular entertainers. Their endorsements can reach a wider audience and lend credibility to the Games. Offer exclusive interviews or content to these influencers to incentivize their participation. Remember, influencer marketing isn't a one-size-fits-all strategy. Carefully select individuals who align with the values and spirit of the Games. Vet their online presence to ensure it aligns with the ethical standards of the Galactic Games Committee. Transparency is key; clearly disclose any partnerships to maintain audience trust.

Develop a comprehensive social media calendar that maps out content releases leading up to, during, and even after the Games. This ensures a consistent flow of information and helps maintain audience interest. Don't just focus on promoting the Games themselves; highlight the stories of the athletes, the history of the sports, and the cultural significance of the event. Develop specific campaigns centered around key moments, like the opening ceremony, major matches, and the closing ceremonies. Prepare pre-written posts, images, and videos in advance to streamline your workflow and ensure timely releases. However, remain flexible. Be prepared to adapt your social media strategy in response to real-time events and trending topics related to the Games. This agility shows your audience that you are engaged and responsive to their interests.

Manage negative feedback constructively. Not every comment will be positive. Have a dedicated team to monitor social media for negative feedback and address concerns promptly and professionally. Turn negative experiences into opportunities for improvement by acknowledging criticisms, offering solutions, and demonstrating a commitment to addressing audience concerns. Establish clear guidelines for your social media team on how to handle negative comments. Empower them to resolve minor issues independently but provide clear escalation paths for dealing with more complex or sensitive situations. Develop a crisis communication plan in case of major controversies or unexpected events that could negatively impact the Games' image on social media. This plan should outline designated spokespersons, pre-approved messaging, and procedures for monitoring and responding to rapidly evolving situations. Remember, social media is a powerful tool that can shape public perception of the Galactic Games. By implementing a well-planned and executed social media strategy, the Galactic Games Committee can create a vibrant online community, build excitement for the event, and ensure its long-term success. This constant monitoring and adaptation ensures the social media strategy remains relevant and effective throughout the duration of the Games.

5.5 Marketing Strategy

The thrill of interstellar competition hinges on effective communication. Reaching potential spectators across the galaxy presents a unique challenge, demanding a multi-pronged approach that considers the diverse cultures and technological landscapes of different civilizations. A successful marketing strategy isn't merely about announcing the games; it's about igniting excitement and fostering a sense of galactic unity through sport. This requires carefully crafted messaging that resonates with each target demographic. Think about the specific appeal of each sport for different species. High-gravity races might captivate dense-bodied creatures, while zero-G ball games could draw in ethereal beings. Tailor promotional materials to these specific interests, highlighting the unique athleticism and spectacle each event offers.

Consider the preferred communication channels of each target audience. Some civilizations might rely on holographic projections, others on telepathic networks, and still others on more traditional broadcast methods. Diversifying your outreach ensures maximum exposure and engagement. Invest in translators and cultural consultants to ensure your message is not only understood but also culturally sensitive and appealing. A poorly translated slogan or an insensitive image could alienate entire populations.

Generating pre-event buzz is crucial for building anticipation. Partner with popular galactic influencers or respected sports figures within various civilizations. Host interactive online events, like virtual reality tours of the sporting venues or Q&A sessions with participating athletes. Offer exclusive behind-the-scenes content to build excitement and generate social media chatter. Remember, the goal is to make the games a must-see event, not just another competition.

Don't neglect traditional media outlets. Establish relationships with galactic news networks and publications. Provide them with press releases, high-quality images, and exclusive interviews with key figures. Offer media partnerships to select outlets, granting them preferential access in exchange for promotional coverage. This symbiotic relationship benefits both parties, ensuring wide dissemination of information while offering exclusive content to dedicated audiences.

Leverage the power of storytelling. Craft narratives around participating athletes, highlighting their journeys, struggles, and triumphs. Showcase the unique aspects of their home planets and cultures, weaving a tapestry of galactic diversity. These stories humanize the athletes, making them relatable and inspiring to audiences across the galaxy. Remember, the Games are not just about competition; they are a celebration of galactic unity and shared experience.

Merchandise plays a vital role in extending the reach of the Games beyond the sporting arenas. Develop a range of high-quality merchandise featuring the Games logo, mascots, and participating teams. Consider offering exclusive items, like limited-edition holographic trading cards or replica sporting equipment. Make merchandise accessible through various channels, including online marketplaces, designated retail outlets, and vending stations at the event venues. This not only generates revenue but also serves as a tangible reminder of the Games, keeping them in the public consciousness long after the closing ceremony.

Implement a robust ticketing system that caters to the diverse needs of a galactic audience. Offer various ticket packages, ranging from single-event access to all-inclusive VIP experiences. Provide secure online purchasing options, accepting multiple forms of galactic currency. Ensure clear and accessible information regarding ticketing procedures, seating arrangements, and venue access. A smooth and efficient ticketing process contributes significantly to a positive spectator experience.

Post-event engagement is essential for maintaining momentum and building anticipation for future Games. Release highlight reels showcasing the most exciting moments of the competition. Conduct post-game interviews with athletes and coaches, capturing their reflections and insights. Share behind-the-scenes footage and exclusive content through social media channels. These activities keep the conversation going, solidifying the Games' position in the galactic sporting calendar.

Finally, data analysis is crucial for measuring the success of your marketing efforts. Track website traffic, social media engagement, and merchandise sales. Analyze audience demographics and identify trends in viewer preferences. This data provides valuable insights into what resonated with your audience and what could be improved for future events. Continuous evaluation and adaptation are essential for maximizing the impact of your marketing strategy and ensuring the continued success of the Galactic Games. By understanding your audience, crafting compelling narratives, and utilizing diverse communication channels, you can effectively market the Games and create a truly unforgettable galactic experience.

6 Chapter 6: Security & Safety

Ensuring the safety and security of a galactic sporting event of this magnitude demands a multi-layered approach, meticulously planned and executed. Consider the sheer diversity of attendees: species with varying physiological needs, differing concepts of personal space, and potentially conflicting cultural norms. This necessitates a security force trained not only in conventional crowd control tactics but also in interspecies diplomacy and conflict resolution. They must be equipped to handle everything from a simple misunderstanding due to language barriers to potential threats from more volatile attendees. This force should be highly visible, acting as both a deterrent and a reassuring presence for participants and spectators alike.

Furthermore, advanced technology plays a crucial role. Think beyond simple metal detectors. Implement bio-scanners capable of detecting concealed weapons, hazardous materials, and even signs of contagious diseases. Utilize real-time monitoring systems that track crowd density and movement, allowing for proactive intervention to prevent potential stampedes or overcrowding, particularly in areas like stadium entrances, concourses, and evacuation routes. These systems should be integrated with sophisticated communication networks that allow for instant coordination between security personnel, medical teams, and event organizers. Consider incorporating drone patrols equipped with thermal imaging and facial recognition software for an added layer of surveillance, particularly in outdoor venues or larger open areas surrounding the main arena.

Emergency planning forms the backbone of any successful security operation, particularly when dealing with an event of interstellar proportions. Develop comprehensive evacuation protocols specific to each venue, taking into account the unique physical characteristics and potential hazards of each location. Establish designated safe zones within and outside the venues, equipped with supplies to accommodate a range of species. These zones must be clearly marked and easily accessible. Conduct regular drills involving security personnel, medical teams, and volunteers to ensure everyone understands their roles and responsibilities in an emergency. Don't overlook the possibility of planetary-specific emergencies. Liaise with local authorities to understand potential natural disasters like seismic activity, extreme weather events, or atmospheric disturbances, and incorporate these risks into your emergency plans.

Beyond physical security, cybersecurity measures are paramount. With so much data being transmitted and stored – from athlete information and ticketing systems to broadcasting feeds and financial transactions – the event is a prime target for cyberattacks. Implement robust encryption protocols to protect sensitive data, and establish a dedicated cybersecurity team to monitor network traffic and respond to any potential breaches. Regular security audits and penetration testing should be conducted in the lead-up to and during the event to identify and address vulnerabilities. Educate staff and volunteers about cybersecurity best practices, emphasizing the importance of strong passwords, phishing awareness, and data protection.

Medical services are another critical component of ensuring participant and spectator safety. Establish fully equipped medical facilities within each venue, staffed by medical professionals experienced in treating a diverse range of species. These facilities should have access to advanced medical technology, including diagnostic imaging, surgical equipment, and life support systems. Ensure sufficient quantities of species-specific medications and antidotes are readily available. Pre-event medical screenings for athletes may be necessary for certain high-risk sports. Beyond the venues, establish designated emergency transport routes and protocols for rapid transfer to off-site medical facilities if needed. Coordinate with local hospitals and medical centers to ensure they have the capacity and resources to handle potential influxes of patients.

Consider the specific needs of different species. Some might require specialized environments, such as controlled atmospheric conditions or specific dietary requirements. Others may have unique communication methods that necessitate the use of translators or specialized communication devices. Cultural sensitivity training for all staff and volunteers is essential to ensure respectful and inclusive interactions with attendees from all corners of the galaxy. Provide clear and concise information about venue accessibility, emergency procedures, and medical services in multiple languages and formats, including visual aids and tactile displays.

Finally, continuous evaluation and improvement are crucial. After each event, conduct a thorough debriefing to identify any security or safety gaps, assess the effectiveness of existing protocols, and incorporate lessons learned into future planning. Stay up-to-date on the latest security technologies and best practices, adapting your strategies to address evolving threats and challenges. By taking a proactive and comprehensive approach to security and safety, you can ensure that the Galactic Games remain a celebration of interstellar sport, free from incident and accessible to all.

6.1   Crowd Control

Effective crowd control at interstellar sporting events presents unique challenges. Consider the sheer diversity of attendees: species with vastly different physical attributes, sensory perceptions, and cultural norms converging in a single location. Understanding these nuances is paramount. Begin by segmenting the expected attendees based on their species' specific needs. For example, Gorthanites, known for their sensitivity to high-frequency sounds, should be seated away from cheering sections and loudspeaker systems. Conversely, the K'tharr, with their enhanced olfactory senses, require ample ventilation and designated aroma-free zones to prevent overstimulation.

Develop comprehensive signage that transcends language barriers. Utilize universally understood symbols and pictograms to direct attendees to designated areas, facilities, and emergency exits. Augment this with holographic projections that display real-time information, adaptable to the specific language of the viewer. These projections can also provide wayfinding assistance, display event schedules, and broadcast important announcements.

Employ a multi-species security force. While robotic security units offer a degree of impartiality and physical strength, having representatives from various attending species fosters trust and facilitates communication. Train these personnel in conflict resolution techniques tailored to interspecies interactions. Equip them with non-lethal crowd control devices, such as sonic repellents calibrated to specific species' sensitivities, and low-gravity containment fields for unruly individuals.

Design the venue with crowd flow in mind. Wide concourses, multiple entry and exit points, and strategically placed rest areas can minimize congestion and prevent bottlenecks. Consider species-specific architectural elements, like elevated platforms for arboreal species or designated low-light zones for nocturnal attendees. Simulate crowd movement patterns using advanced software, incorporating variables like species-specific locomotion and behavioral tendencies, to optimize venue layout and prevent potential hazards.

Establish clear codes of conduct. Communicate these guidelines pre-event through official channels, including galactic registration portals and species-specific communication networks. Outline expected behaviors, prohibited items, and the consequences of non-compliance. Ensure that these regulations are enforced consistently and fairly by the multi-species security force.

Prepare for unexpected events. Develop comprehensive emergency protocols, including evacuation procedures tailored to different species' needs. Establish designated safe zones equipped with species-specific life support systems and medical supplies. Conduct regular drills involving both security personnel and event staff to ensure a coordinated response in the event of a security breach, natural disaster, or medical emergency.

Integrate technology seamlessly. Utilize biometric scanning at entry points to verify attendee credentials and prevent unauthorized access. Implement real-time crowd monitoring systems that track attendee density, movement patterns, and potential flashpoints. Deploy drones equipped with thermal imaging and behavioral analysis software to identify potential security threats and proactively address developing situations.

Consider cultural sensitivities. Certain species may have specific rituals or customs related to large gatherings. Accommodate these practices where possible, providing designated areas for prayer, meditation, or other culturally significant activities. Engage cultural advisors from different species to ensure that the event respects the diverse traditions of the attendees.

Promote positive interactions. Organize pre-event cultural exchange programs that allow attendees from different species to interact and learn about each other's customs. Foster a sense of community and shared experience through interactive displays, collaborative art projects, and friendly competitions. These initiatives can help break down barriers and create a more inclusive and welcoming environment for all attendees.

Remember, effective crowd control is not merely about preventing chaos. It's about creating a safe, enjoyable, and culturally sensitive experience for every attendee, regardless of their species of origin. By embracing diversity and planning proactively, you can ensure a successful and memorable event for all. Through meticulous planning and thoughtful execution, the Games can be a showcase of galactic unity, celebrating both competition and camaraderie. This proactive approach builds trust and fosters a sense of shared responsibility for the event's success, ultimately contributing to a more positive and harmonious experience for everyone involved.

6.2 Emergency Plans

No sporting event, especially one of galactic proportions, can afford to overlook comprehensive emergency planning. This chapter provides a detailed framework for anticipating, mitigating, and responding to potential crises during the Galactic Games. From minor incidents to major catastrophes, preparedness is key to ensuring the safety and well-being of all involved. We'll explore specific protocols, communication strategies, and resource allocation necessary for a swift and effective response to a range of emergencies. This isn't just about ticking boxes; it's about safeguarding lives and preserving the integrity of the Games themselves.

First and foremost, a robust risk assessment is crucial. Identify potential hazards unique to the chosen planet and sporting venues. Consider environmental factors like seismic activity, extreme weather patterns, or the presence of indigenous flora and fauna that could pose a threat. Analyze the potential for technological malfunctions within the arena, transportation systems, and broadcasting infrastructure. Evaluate the risks associated with large crowds of diverse species, accounting for cultural sensitivities and potential interspecies conflicts. A thorough risk assessment forms the backbone of any effective emergency plan.

Once potential hazards are identified, develop specific protocols for each scenario. These protocols should outline clear chains of command, detailing who is responsible for what in each type of emergency. Establish evacuation procedures for the stadium and surrounding areas, considering different mobility needs and species-specific requirements. Designate safe zones and assembly points easily accessible to all attendees. Implement a robust communication system capable of disseminating real-time information to participants, spectators, and emergency personnel in multiple languages and formats. Regular drills and simulations are essential for testing these protocols, ensuring that all personnel are well-trained and prepared to act swiftly and efficiently.

Medical emergencies will require specialized consideration. Establish fully equipped medical facilities within the venue, staffed with medical professionals experienced in treating a variety of species. Ensure adequate supplies of medical equipment and pharmaceuticals, taking into account species-specific physiological differences. Coordinate with local planetary medical services to establish emergency transport protocols to off-site facilities if needed. Pre-event medical screenings for athletes may be necessary for certain high-risk sports, and medical personnel should be strategically positioned throughout the venue to provide immediate assistance.

Security breaches and acts of aggression are another potential concern in a large-scale interstellar event. Develop a comprehensive security plan that incorporates advanced surveillance technology, trained security personnel, and clear protocols for responding to various security threats. Establish communication channels with local law enforcement and planetary security forces. Consider implementing screening procedures at venue entrances to detect and prevent the entry of prohibited items. Regular security assessments and vulnerability analyses should be conducted to adapt to evolving threats and ensure the ongoing safety of all involved.

In the event of a planetary-scale emergency, such as a natural disaster, a separate evacuation plan is necessary. This plan should include coordinated transportation to off-world locations, utilizing pre-arranged agreements with interstellar transport providers. Establish emergency shelters on nearby planets with the capacity to accommodate a large influx of refugees. Coordinate with planetary authorities to ensure the smooth execution of this plan, and establish clear communication channels to keep attendees informed of the situation and provide instructions for evacuation.

Effective communication is paramount in any emergency. Establish a multi-tiered communication system incorporating redundant channels to ensure message delivery even in the event of infrastructure failure. Designate a central communication hub responsible for coordinating information flow and disseminating updates to relevant parties. Utilize a variety of communication methods, including real-time alerts to personal devices, public address systems, holographic projections, and dedicated emergency broadcast channels. Pre-translated messages in multiple languages should be readily available to ensure clear and timely communication with a diverse audience.

Resource allocation is another critical component of emergency preparedness. Establish a dedicated emergency fund to cover unforeseen expenses related to crisis response. Secure agreements with suppliers of essential resources, such as food, water, medical supplies, and temporary shelter. Develop a logistics plan for the efficient distribution of these resources in the event of an emergency. Consider establishing backup power sources for critical infrastructure and communication systems. Proper resource management ensures a swift and effective response, minimizing the impact of any unforeseen event.

Finally, post-event analysis is essential for continuous improvement. After any emergency, conduct a thorough review of the response, identifying areas of success and areas for improvement. Gather feedback from participants, spectators, and emergency personnel to gain valuable insights. Update emergency plans and protocols based on lessons learned. This iterative process ensures that the Galactic Games' emergency preparedness continually evolves to meet the challenges of this unique interstellar event. By prioritizing safety and preparedness, we not only protect lives but also ensure the long-term success and sustainability of the Games. Remember, comprehensive planning is not an expense; it's an investment in the future of galactic sports.

6.3 Medical Services

Ensuring the well-being of all participants in the Galactic Games demands a comprehensive medical framework. This encompasses preventative measures, emergency response protocols, and specialized care considerations for the diverse species competing. Establishing robust medical services is not merely a logistical necessity; it is a demonstration of the Games' commitment to the value of every athlete's life and health. This commitment underscores the ethical responsibility inherent in hosting an event of this magnitude and galactic diversity.

Consider the sheer breadth of physiological differences represented at the Games. Athletes hailing from low-gravity environments might experience skeletal stress in a higher-gravity venue. Respiratory systems adapted to methane atmospheres require specialized life support equipment during competition. Even seemingly minor differences, such as variations in optimal body temperature or dietary requirements, can significantly impact performance and well-being if not adequately addressed. Therefore, a detailed medical profile for each participating athlete is essential, outlining species-specific needs, pre-existing conditions, and emergency contact information. This database should be readily accessible to medical personnel throughout the Games.

Beyond individual athlete profiles, dedicated medical facilities are crucial. These facilities should be strategically located throughout the venue, equipped to handle a range of medical situations, from minor injuries to life-threatening emergencies. Real-time translation services are paramount, enabling clear communication between medical staff and athletes who might not share a common language. Furthermore, medical teams should include specialists familiar with the unique physiologies of different galactic species, ensuring culturally sensitive and effective treatment. Consider, for example, a species whose nervous system operates on bioluminescent signals; a physician unfamiliar with this could misinterpret physiological responses, leading to inaccurate diagnoses and potentially harmful treatments.

Emergency protocols must account for the diverse nature of the Games. Evacuation plans should consider varying mobility needs, environmental sensitivities, and potential communication barriers. Designated medical transport, equipped with species-specific life support systems, must be readily available. Pre-arranged agreements with local hospitals and medical specialists outside the venue can provide additional support for complex cases. Regular drills and simulations involving medical personnel, security teams, and venue staff are essential to ensure smooth execution in a real emergency. Imagine a scenario where a sudden atmospheric fluctuation within the arena impacts athletes with sensitive respiratory systems;

a well-rehearsed emergency protocol can be the difference between a minor incident and a major catastrophe.

Doping control requires specialized adaptation for interstellar competition. Substances considered performance-enhancing for one species might be essential for the survival of another. Therefore, the anti-doping program must be carefully designed in consultation with experts in xenopharmacology and species-specific physiology. Clear guidelines and education programs are essential to ensure fairness and transparency, while also respecting the physiological needs of all athletes. Regular testing using advanced detection methods can deter potential violations and maintain the integrity of the Games. A robust appeals process is also necessary to address any disputed results and ensure due process for all athletes.

Beyond competition, preventative measures play a vital role in maintaining athlete health. Regular health screenings can identify potential issues early on. Nutritional guidelines tailored to different species' dietary needs should be provided. Mental health support services, recognizing the stress and pressure of interstellar competition, must also be accessible. These services should consider cultural differences in how mental health is perceived and addressed, ensuring culturally sensitive and effective care. Providing a holistic approach to athlete well-being not only enhances performance but also fosters a positive and supportive environment for all participants.

Finally, collaboration with intergalactic medical organizations can significantly enhance the quality and comprehensiveness of medical services.

Sharing knowledge and best practices can lead to the development of new medical technologies and treatment protocols tailored for interstellar athletes. This collaboration can also facilitate the training of medical personnel specializing in interspecies care, creating a network of experts capable of addressing the unique medical challenges of future Galactic Games. The establishment of a dedicated medical advisory board, comprising representatives from different galactic sectors, can ensure ongoing review and improvement of medical services, reflecting the evolving needs of interstellar competition. This ongoing commitment to medical excellence safeguards the health and well-being of the athletes, upholding the highest ethical standards for the Galactic Games and reinforcing their significance as a celebration of unity and sporting achievement across the galaxy.

7 Chapter 7: Post-Event Proce-dures

The echoing cheers of the final match have faded, the last shimmering transport ship has blinked into hyperspace, and the colossal stadium now stands silent, a monument to the recently concluded games. This, how-ever, does not mark the end of the Galactic Games Committee's respon-sibilities. A significant phase remains: the meticulous execution of post-event procedures. This crucial stage ensures the event's legacy, maintains financial transparency, and paves the way for future interstellar competi-tions. It is a time for reflection, analysis, and meticulous record-keeping.

The culmination of the Galactic Games demands a celebration of athleti-cism and sportsmanship: the Awards Ceremony. This ceremony requires careful orchestration. Consider the diverse cultural protocols of the par-ticipating species. Trophy designs should be universally appealing, avoid-ing symbols with potentially negative connotations in certain galactic cul-tures. Translation services must be impeccable, ensuring accurate and re-spectful communication during the presentations. The venue for the cere-mony should accommodate the varying physical sizes and environmental needs of the attendees. Live broadcasts should be meticulously planned, capturing the emotion of the moment and transmitting it across the galaxy. Remember, this ceremony is the final impression of the games for many, and its success will significantly impact the perception of the event as a whole.

Beyond the celebratory fanfare, the Committee must finalize the comprehensive financial reports. This process involves consolidating all income streams, from sponsorship deals and merchandising revenue to ticket sales and broadcasting rights. A detailed breakdown of expenditures, including venue rental, security personnel, medical supplies, and athlete accommodations, must be meticulously documented. This financial transparency is crucial for accountability to sponsors, stakeholders, and the galactic community at large. Discrepancies must be thoroughly investigated and explained, ensuring the integrity of the Games. Furthermore, this financial data provides invaluable insights for future events, allowing for more accurate budgeting and resource allocation.

An independent audit of the financial records should be conducted to ensure impartiality and accuracy. The chosen auditing firm must be reputable and experienced in handling interstellar transactions and multi-currency accounting. Their report should be publicly accessible, demonstrating the Committee's commitment to transparency and responsible financial management. This builds trust within the galactic community and reinforces the legitimacy of the Games.

The dissemination of these reports is equally crucial. They should be made available not only to sponsors and stakeholders but also to the public through official channels. This demonstrates accountability and provides valuable insights into the financial complexities of organizing an event of this magnitude. Consider different formats for the report, including interactive data visualizations, to make the information more accessible and engaging for a wider audience. Accompanying the financial data should be a narrative report, summarizing the key achievements and challenges of the Games, providing context for the numbers.

Following the dissemination of the financial reports, the Committee should conduct a comprehensive post-event evaluation. This involves gathering feedback from various stakeholders, including athletes, spectators, sponsors, and media representatives. Surveys, interviews, and focus groups can be utilized to collect data on all aspects of the event, from venue accessibility and security measures to the quality of the broadcasting and the overall spectator experience. This feedback is invaluable for identifying areas for improvement in future games.

Analyzing the collected data involves identifying recurring themes and patterns in the feedback. This analysis should be objective and data-driven, focusing on actionable insights rather than subjective opinions. The results of this analysis should be compiled into a detailed report, outlining specific recommendations for future events. This report will serve as a blueprint for continuous improvement, ensuring that each iteration of the Galactic Games builds upon the successes and learns from the challenges of its predecessors. This meticulous approach to post-event procedures is not merely a formality; it is a critical investment in the future of the Galactic Games. By embracing transparency, accountability, and continuous improvement, the Committee ensures the longevity and prestige of this interstellar spectacle.

7.1 Awards Ceremony

The culmination of any interstellar sporting event is the awards ceremony. This is not merely a formality; it's a celebration of athleticism, sportsmanship, and the unifying power of competition across the galaxy. It's the Galactic Games Committee's responsibility to ensure this ceremony reflects the grandeur of the games themselves and leaves a lasting positive impression on participants and spectators alike. Planning for this event should begin well in advance, ideally concurrent with the initial stages of event organization.

The first crucial element is selecting an appropriate venue. While the closing ceremony might take place in the main arena, a separate, more intimate venue can offer a distinct celebratory atmosphere. Consider a location with ample space for award presentations, seating for dignitaries, athletes, and invited guests, and robust technological infrastructure to support holographic displays and interstellar broadcasts. Accessibility for diverse species, including gravitational adjustments and atmospheric controls, must also be factored in.

The award categories themselves must be clearly defined. Traditional categories such as gold, silver, and bronze medals for individual and team events are a standard. Consider, however, incorporating awards that recognize outstanding sportsmanship, exceptional performance in a specific skill, or contributions to interstellar unity through sport. Design and production of the physical awards should be commissioned from reputable artisans, ensuring they are visually striking and incorporate materials representative of the diverse cultures participating in the games. Remember, these awards will become cherished symbols of achievement, displayed across the galaxy.

The ceremony's program should be carefully curated to be both engaging and respectful of the time commitments of attendees. Proclamations from dignitaries, representing key galactic sectors, should be concise and focused on the unifying power of the games. Musical performances, showcasing diverse artistic traditions from across the galaxy, can add a vibrant and celebratory dimension. Holographic displays, recapping the highlights of the games, can evoke emotional resonance and serve as a lasting memento of the event.

Logistics for the awards ceremony are paramount. A clear protocol for award presentation should be established, outlining the procession of athletes, the announcement of winners, and the dignitaries responsible for bestowing the honors. Consider the cultural nuances of different species regarding physical contact and forms of acknowledgement. Translators should be available to ensure all participants understand the proceedings, and real-time closed captioning for interstellar broadcasts should be incorporated.

Behind the scenes, dedicated teams are necessary to manage the smooth flow of the ceremony. A team responsible for athlete coordination ensures participants are properly attired, understand the protocol, and arrive at the designated areas on time. A technical crew manages the audio-visual elements, ensuring flawless execution of holographic displays, sound systems, and broadcast feeds. Security personnel, discreetly integrated into the event, maintain order and address any unforeseen circumstances.

Post-ceremony procedures should be considered in the planning stages. A designated area for post-ceremony media interactions allows athletes to share their experiences with the galactic press. Secure transportation should be arranged for athletes returning to their respective delegations or accommodations. Finally, a comprehensive archive of the ceremony, including recordings, photographs, and transcripts, should be created for historical preservation and future reference.

The awards ceremony is the capstone of the Galactic Games, a moment of collective celebration and recognition. By meticulously planning and executing this event, the Galactic Games Committee not only honors the athletes but also reinforces the values of sportsmanship, intercultural understanding, and galactic unity that are at the heart of these games. It's the final impression, the lasting memory – and it deserves the utmost attention to detail. Remember, the success of this ceremony echoes across the galaxy, impacting future participation and the legacy of the Games themselves. Therefore, a well-executed awards ceremony is not just an end, but a powerful beginning. It's the spark that ignites anticipation for the next

Galactic Games, a testament to the enduring spirit of competition and the power of sport to unite the galaxy. Every element, from the smallest detail to the grandest spectacle, contributes to this final, resonating message.

The presentation of awards should be a dignified affair, reflecting the importance of the achievements being recognized. Consider the order of presentation, starting perhaps with less competitive categories and culminating with the most prestigious awards. Announcing the nominees before revealing the winner can build suspense and highlight the accomplishments of all finalists. Prepare brief biographical sketches of each winner to be read during the presentation, emphasizing their dedication, training, and journey to the Galactic Games.

Incorporate elements of cultural exchange and understanding throughout the ceremony. Showcase the unique traditions and artistic expressions of different galactic civilizations through music, dance, or holographic storytelling. This not only adds richness and diversity to the event but also fosters mutual respect and appreciation among participants and spectators from different corners of the galaxy.

Finally, don't underestimate the power of symbolism. The imagery used in the ceremony, the design of the awards, and the messages conveyed by dignitaries should all reinforce the themes of unity, sportsmanship, and the pursuit of excellence. These symbolic elements will resonate with audiences long after the ceremony concludes, leaving a lasting impression of the Galactic Games as a force for positive change in the galaxy.

7.2 Financial Reports

The shimmer of the closing ceremony fireworks still dances in the committee's collective memory, yet the real work begins now: reconciling the galactic ledger. A comprehensive financial report, meticulously compiled and transparently presented, is the cornerstone of a successful interstellar sporting event. It demonstrates fiscal responsibility to sponsors, justifies expenditures to governing bodies, and provides valuable data for future events. This process, while complex, is manageable when approached systematically. Begin by collating all financial records. These include pre-event budget proposals, sponsorship agreements, vendor invoices, ticket sales data, merchandise revenue, and any unforeseen expense reports. Organize these documents by category and chronology, ensuring easy access and cross-referencing.

Remember that interstellar currencies fluctuate. Establish a baseline currency for all transactions and meticulously convert all income and expenses to this standard. Document the exchange rates used at each transaction point, maintaining a record for audit purposes. This is crucial for accurately reflecting the financial health of the event and avoiding discrepancies later on. Discrepancies arising from currency fluctuations should be explained with supporting documentation from recognized galactic exchange authorities.

Next, categorize expenditures. Create detailed breakdowns for each major cost center: venue rental, infrastructure development, personnel costs, athlete accommodation and transport, security provisions, broadcasting rights, marketing campaigns, medical services, and contingency funds. Within each category, itemize specific expenses, attaching supporting documentation. For example, within "Athlete Accommodation and Transport," detail costs for interstellar shuttles, planetary lodging, and per diem allowances. This level of granularity enables precise analysis and identifies areas for potential cost optimization in future events.

Revenue streams must be documented with equal precision. Categorize income from ticket sales (distinguishing between different seating tiers and event days), merchandising, broadcasting rights, sponsorships, and any other sources. Scrutinize contracts with sponsors, ensuring all promised payments have been received and accounted for. If revenue falls short of projections, analyze the potential causes – was attendance lower than anticipated? Did merchandise sales underperform? – and document these findings for future planning.

Once all income and expenditures are meticulously categorized and converted, generate a comprehensive summary report. This report should present a clear overview of the event's financial performance, highlighting key metrics such as total revenue, total expenditure, net profit or loss, return on investment for sponsors, and a breakdown of expenses by category. Accompany the summary with detailed supporting schedules that provide the granular data backing up the overarching figures. This allows stakeholders to delve deeper into specific areas of interest and understand the financial narrative of the event.

Transparency is paramount. Ensure your financial report adheres to the Galactic Games Committee's established accounting principles and reporting standards. Engage an independent auditor, preferably one with interstellar experience, to verify the accuracy and completeness of your financial records. This external validation bolsters credibility and assures stakeholders of the report's integrity. Furthermore, consider presenting the report in multiple formats – holographic projections, downloadable data files, and physical copies – to cater to the diverse technological preferences of your galactic audience.

Finally, don't just file the report away. Analyze it. Identify areas of financial success and areas needing improvement. Were certain expenditures unexpectedly high? Could revenue streams be diversified or optimized? These insights are invaluable for future event planning. Document the lessons learned, both financial and logistical, and share these with the broader Galactic Games Committee community. This collective learning process contributes to the ongoing success and sustainability of interstellar sporting events. Consider the report a living document, a testament to the hard work and dedication that went into the event, and a roadmap for even grander spectacles in the future. Remember, the final whistle doesn't mark the end of the game; it signals the start of a new cycle of planning, improvement, and reaching for the stars.

www.ingramcontent.com/pod-product-compliance
Ingram Content Group UK Ltd.
Pitfield, Milton Keynes, MK11 3LW, UK
UKHW021431230125
4262UKWH00029B/543